INTERPRETING YOUR TONGUES

**EFFECTIVE KEYS FOR UNLOCKING
THE CODED VOICE OF GOD
WHEN SPEAKING IN TONGUES**

PETER TOWONGO

ISBN: 978-0-9949361-2-7

Unless otherwise indicated all Scriptures quoted are taken from the King James Version (KJV): KING JAMES VERSION, public domain.

In this book the name "satan" or "devil" is written in lowercase to purposely discredit him even to the point of breaking grammatical laws on proper nouns.

Ordering Information:
www.compassionministry.org | www.petertowongo.com
info@petertowongo.com | towongopeter@yahoo.com

Printed in the United States of America

TABLE OF CONTENTS

DEDICATION

*This book is dedicated to those
aspiring to walk in the supernatural
with power and might.*

ENDORSEMENTS

Do you want to speak the mysteries of God? Peter's book, *Interpreting Your Tongues,* will unlock the mysteries of the amazing gift of tongues and learn to release God's power from within.

Rev. Dr. Carrie Wachsmann
Author and mentor, *Wachsmann Communications*

The gift of tongues and interpretation of tongues are relevant to the church, because they edify, convict, and identify the true believer. The author in this work seeks to introduce the believer to the gift. Understanding the gifts of the Spirit, and the Person of the Holy Spirit require a lifetime of study and experience. This work is like a roadmap. I pray that you enjoy the journey.

Rev. Dr. John S. Peters
Pastor and founder, *Gentle Rain Fellowship of Faith*

Speaking and interpretation of tongues are some of the most controversial topics in Christianity. It is very important for every believer to know the importance of tongues interpretation. *Interpreting Your Tongues* is a great book which will help you to understand the mysteries behind tongues.

Rev. Richmond Donkor
Pastor and author, *The Restored House Chapel Ministries*

ACKNOWLEDGEMENTS

All honor and glory go to our Father in heaven for His great love in sending Jesus Christ to die on the Cross as our substitute. He added me in the list of those who have accepted His salvation call through the enablement of the Holy Ghost. Otherwise, I would have been a naught.

Furthermore, the Holy Spirit does an overwhelming advocacy—He actually "sponsored" the keys in this book you will shortly use to decode the coded voice of God hidden in tongues. Without His counsel, you wouldn't have this book.

I would also be remiss if I don't mention and thank Reverend Gwen Dreger for introducing an important book-writing workshop featuring Dr. Mike Smalley. Thank you Dr. Smalley for directing my knowledge on precision.

Much appreciation goes to Reverend Dr. John S. Peters who unwaveringly accepted to write the Foreword of this book making it commendable to vast spheres. To Pastor Richmond Donkor for adding your endorsement, and my editorial team, Dr. Win Wachsmann and Dr. Carrie Wachsmann, you have done a remarkable work editing and designing both the interior and cover of this book. Thank you so much.

In addition, a number of notable ministers of God, mentors and friends including my family have been instrumental in shaping my life making it ready for the supernatural. Space wouldn't accommodate all your names and contributions but I have treasured them in my heart.

Lastly, my compliments go to those in my centres of influence for their questions concerning the enigmas of tongues which enabled me to spend quality time investigating the phenomenon and then writing this book.

Peter Towongo

Canada 2017

FOREWORD

Greetings and salutations in that great and mighty name of Jesus, who is the Christ and our elder brother through the adoption process initiated by the shedding of His own blood for the redemption of our souls. Praise be to God forever more!

It is my pleasure and privilege to once again write the Foreword for my brother in Christ. I have served God for more than 30 years in the ministry of His Word, and have been the author of *The Sojourners' Guide to Knowing Jesus, Understanding the Lord's Prayer, Equipping the Saints,* and *A World in Transition.*

Like so many others, Peter Towongo has had a long and arduous journey, and has overcome many difficulties along the way. In other words, his faith has been tested and tried, and God has brought him through, to be a light and a guide for others.

In this book, *Interpreting You Tongues,* Peter introduces us to a topic from the Bible which has been misunderstood, misused, and often vilified in the same manner Jesus Christ was crucified. Speaking in tongues is a gift from the Holy Ghost, and is vital to the work of the church and saints.

When the Holy Spirit was poured out upon the saints in the upper room in Jerusalem, four things happened. The first thing that happened was a "sound" that was heard throughout the city, as of a mighty rushing wind. This drew a very large crowd to the building where the Holy Spirit fell. The second thing that happened was that "cloven tongues like as of fire" appeared over the head of each believer gathered in the upper room.

The third thing that happened was that every man and woman "spoke in other tongues" that they had not premeditated. The fourth thing that happened is that everyone in the crowd below "heard" them speaking in the tongues of neighboring and faraway countries. The result of this phenomenon was that three thousand souls were added to the kingdom of God that very hour.

The gift of interpretation of tongues is one of the nine gifts of the Holy Spirit. It is the companion gift to the gift of tongues, and we see it written in the Bible as tongues, and the interpretation of tongues.

The Bible tells us that tongues and interpretation of tongues add up or equal to prophecy.

Finally, the gift of tongues and interpretation of tongues are relevant to the church, because they edify, convict, and identify the true believer.

The author in this work seeks to introduce the believer to the gift. Understanding the gifts of the Spirit, and the Person of the Holy Spirit require a lifetime of study and experience. This work is like a roadmap, I pray that you enjoy the journey.

Rev. Dr. John S. Peters
Pastor and founder, *Gentle Rain Fellowship of Faith*

INTRODUCTION

This book is not intended to be a model to make you an "expert" in interpreting the tongues of *other* believers. It's rather a personal enrichment intended to help you decode the coded voice of God when *you* speak in tongues. It also provides some amazing "bonuses" that would enable you to hear God clearly through means of special transactions with the Lord other than by tongues.

If you could ever think as to why many Christians today stumble in life, quit ministries and stay in zones unprotected by the shadow of the Almighty, you would probably discover that they often miss the voice of God even though some of them speak in tongues. Yes, they can speak in tongues, experience the presence of God and yet spiritual blindness seems to have overshadowed them. They fail to walk in accordance to the plan of God because they find it difficult to hear directives from God or interpret their own tongues.

In the trend of Christian writings today, *Interpreting Your Tongues* stands unique. It reveals hidden enigmas in tongues that have often been flouted and yet it's one of the mysterious ways God communicates urgent matters to believers.

This book gives guidance to hear God talking to you as you speak in tongues. The moment you discover these secrets you won't reject tongues utterance—you will always remain in the secret place.

If you have not yet spoken in tongues by the Spirit of the Lord, this book will help you activate your tongues. The prerequisite for tongues is to *first* accept Jesus Christ into your life and then develop a burning desire to receive the gift.

Part one of this book unpacks the secrets behind tongues that are beneficial to our lives. When we speak in tongues, we utter mysteries that the mind cannot comprehend. For the Bible says "he that speaketh in an unknown tongue speaketh not unto men, but unto God: for no man understandeth him; howbeit in the spirit he speaketh mysteries." (1 Cor. 14:2)

The message obtained in tongues is manufactured within the faculty of the *renewed* human spirit and then released directly without the "filters" of the mind.

The mind is purposely avoided for its carnality; unless otherwise it is interpreted, no one would decode its meaning.

Speaking in tongues builds the one speaking and assures him of the secure salvation he has obtained in Jesus Christ. When the tongue is interpreted it becomes a prophecy to you and to those listening thus edifying the church. It also convicts sinners to turn to Jesus Christ because they are able to see the works of God in ordinary believers.

Satan is troubled a lot because tongues avoid him. He cannot hear whatever is spoken and is caught off guard. All his monitoring spirits daring to monitor believers in order to frustrate their plans will hear nothing since the spoken words are coded. When you wage war, satan is caught unprepared and will lose the battle against your life.

Part two of this book unearths proven ways to interpret your "own" tongues as you go on speaking. This is a part that demands careful attention. I have come across many believers telling me they "tried" asking God to give them the gift of interpretation of tongues but to no avail. Remember, if we don't listen carefully to someone speaking to us, we can miss what he is saying. Learn and seek the gift, for you will find it.

After reading this part, you will be surprised to realize

that God keeps talking to you in your own tongues for some time even if you keep ignoring His signs, symbols, words, statements and flushes revealing great trend of answers.

The last part of this book helps us to activate the gift of tongues to the point where power and prophecy are easily realized. Those who speak in tongues will be stirred to enjoy the gift. Those who struggle to be filled in the Spirit will find encouragements to help them get connected with the Holy Spirit and begin to speak in tongues for their first time and then continuously.

If there are blockages hindering the Spirit of God from operating in your life, the book will provide the means to help overcome those blockages through the *rhema* you will soon receive as you keep reading.

I wish you the best as you continue reading this important book of its kind. It's my prayer that you will be filled in the power of the Holy Ghost and continue to speak in tongues for the glory of God. Shalom!

PART I

UNPACKING TONGUES

CHAPTER 1

TONGUES EDIFY BELIEVERS

Have you ever wondered why some people uphold certain ideas in which you have no interest? What prompted them to embrace those things in which you don't see any value? Is there anything hidden within that you have not yet figured out to make you embrace those things?

Speaking in tongues is one of the New Testament's blessings for the church and yet it has been sidelined by many. Truly, any believer who is filled with the Spirit of God does enjoy speaking in tongues. "Something" is building him up thus prompting him to rely on the power of the Holy Ghost at all times.

Theologians call the phenomenon of speaking in tongues *glossolalia,* a term derived from the Greek phrase *glossais lalos*—meaning to speak in, with, or by tongues. Unlike the Old Testament which was written in Hebrew, the New Testament was however written in Greek since Greek was the official language of the Land at that time. Therefore, glossolalia or speaking in tongues is a speech-like expression, but lacks comprehensive intelligence to the one speaking and those listening unless otherwise it is divinely interpreted.

The other related Greek word to glossolalia is *xenolalia* where a *real* language is spoken in tongues but unknown to the one speaking. If there are people around who speak that language they can understand everything. (Acts 2:6)

On the other hand, during the time Peter and John were arrested by the priests and Sadducees, they were warned not to preach in the name of Jesus. But they refused to heed to their warnings, instead returned to their own (church) and began to channel diverse kinds of prayers to the Father.

The Holy Spirit came mightily and stirred them up for even greater exploits. "And when they had prayed, the place was shaken where they were assembled together; and they were all filled with the Holy Ghost, and they spake the word of God with boldness." (Acts 4:31)

Where did they get that power which enabled them to defy all odds? It came from *within* them as they worshipped the Father in the Spirit and truth. For Jesus says, anyone "...who believes in Me, as the Scripture has said, *out of his heart* will flow rivers of living water." (John 7:38 emphasis italicized)

EDIFICATION OF THE SPEAKER THROUGH TONGUES

The book of 1 Corinthians 14:4 assures us that speaking in tongues brings personal edification: "He that speaketh in an unknown tongue edifieth himself." The Greek root word for edification Paul uses here is *oikodome* which connotes building up of a believer or promoting growth in Christian holiness, wisdom, piety or happiness.

So when speaking in tongues, the one speaking is building himself up thus exerting divine power for courage, holiness, boldness and all aspects of supernatural endowments. It is like boosting a car battery that has run low. Unless the battery is boosted, it cannot emit enough electricity to start the engine.

Speaking in tongues boosts you up, connects you with your inner man and the Spirit of God to transmit divine electricity all over your body that is so refreshing.

The Bible has given us some clues concerning two interesting personalities that are involved when praying or speaking in tongues—the Holy Spirit and the human spirit. It is the Holy Spirit trying to communicate with the speaker's spirit to saturate the soul and body with divine power and peace.

For example, if the one speaking is in a desperate condition the Spirit of God knows exactly what the speaker needs and then the Holy Spirit asks the Father to provide the needed element. If the person is intimidated by satan, the Holy Spirit asks the Father to send boldness to the speaker. But remember all these "transmissions" are done in a mysterious manner unknown to the speaker unless otherwise interpreted.

When the early church was intimidated by satan and the religious leaders to stop preaching Jesus Christ and perform His miracles, they had to pray for supernatural endowment which enabled them to speak the word of God with boldness.

But today, any minor intimidation that some preachers encounter, hits them so hard that many of them become so discouraged and frustrated, and hence they abandon the mission God wants them to fulfill.

The reason could be that many of these ministers are not filled with the Holy Spirit or they don't exercise their tongues regularly.

Praying in tongues changes the atmosphere for the better. We get hurt every day since we live in this world where the devil operates. So if satan hurts you through others, don't let your anger bog you down to make you sin. The best solution to revive your spirit is to *forgive* those who allowed the devil to use them as his instruments and then *destroy* the contaminated situation by speaking in tongues.

Remember when Paul and Silas were jailed. Instead of wailing and gnashing their teeth, they worshiped God and prayed (of course in tongues too). The result was their chains were broken and prison doors opened. (Acts 16:25-27)

Just imagine how happy they were on seeing the breaking of their chains and the opening of the prison door. They were indeed edified and instead preached to their jailer and led his family to Christ.

When we pray in tongues for self-edification, certain things happen—we receive power, encouragement and boldness. We will be able to hear God clearly and know His intentions since the overflow of His anointing is soaking our speech including our body.

Speaking in tongues assures us that our salvation is *intact* with God. We experience certain movements within our inner man. If you speak in tongues, you receive power proving the presence of God is within you. You don't doubt whether you are saved or not— you are edified indeed!

EDIFICATION OF THE CHURCH THROUGH TONGUES

To profoundly understand speaking in tongues in terms of edification, these phrases "speaking in tongues," "praying in tongues", "praying with the spirit" and "praying in the Spirit" need to be carefully observed.

Many Christians get confused by these terms. Others believe that speaking in tongues, praying in tongues, praying *with* the spirit and praying *in* the Spirit are synonymous—they carry the same meaning and same connotation. Well, let's look closely to the few of these verses to help us see their intended intentions. We will bold and italicize those words or phrases we are focusing on to divulge their meaning.

Acts 2:4 reveals that the believers at the upper room during the Pentecost day "were all filled with the Holy Ghost, and began to **speak with other tongues**, as the Spirit gave them utterance."

"For if I **pray in an unknown tongue**, my spirit prayeth, but my understanding is unfruitful." (1 Cor. 14:14) "What is it then? I will **pray with the spirit**, and I will pray with the understanding also: I will sing with the spirit, and I will sing with the understanding also." (v.15)

"And ***pray in the Spirit*** on all occasions with all kinds of prayers and requests. With this in mind, be alert and always keep on praying for all the Lord's people." (Eph. 6:18) "But ye, beloved, building up yourselves on your most holy faith, ***praying in the Holy Ghost***." (Jude 1:20)

The supernatural endowment of tongues for believers involves the Spirit of God, the human spirit and our faculties that infuse vocalization.

Therefore, *speaking* in tongues connotes prophetic sayings downloaded from the throne of Grace while *praying* in tongues emphasizes the nature of our communication with God through tongues.

On the other hand, praying with the *spirit* with a lower case "s" refers to the kind of prayers that come from the human spirit with the spirit's way of communication. Similarly praying in the *Spirit* with upper case "S" refers to the intercession of the Holy Spirit within us through tongues or groanings.

We will now explain tongues in relation to the edification of the church as a whole.

Speaking in Tongues

Speaking in tongues is a prophecy in nature that has been hidden mysteriously unless it is unpacked for the benefit of those listening otherwise they won't understand anything. The English word *speak* literally means to say something or convey information to someone or in other times to reprove or advise someone in certain matters so that intended results are attained.

Therefore, when a person speaks in tongues before a congregation *there is a message from God that is to be conveyed to them or to particular persons within the church.* That is why Paul is saying here that tongues hide prophecies and these prophecies have to be emptied so that they can edify the whole body of Christ. Thus he says, "he that speaketh with tongues, except he interpret, that the church may receive edifying." (I Cor. 14:5)

Also, when someone addresses the congregation by speaking in tongues other than the common language known by the listeners, someone has to interpret it. If not, then the tongues speaker should hold their peace to avoid confusion. If two or more people have a word to the church in tongues, it should be done orderly—one speaks after the other, not all at once. Unless otherwise it is praying in tongues or with the spirit that is siphoned towards heaven, not the church. Let us also be aware that when speaking in tongues, we can be airing *known* or *unknown* languages. Paul says, "Though I speak with the tongues of men and of angels...." (1 Cor. 13:1) The revelation here implies that speaking in *tongues of men* is actually speaking "known" language(s) spoken by certain groups of people on earth. However, speaking in *tongues of angels* is essentially speaking mysterious language(s) "unknown" to mankind but known to angels.

This reminds me of a minister preaching in a church in Toronto, Canada. He began to speak in tongues. Suddenly a woman jumped from her seat celebrating. When asked, she said her daughter was a missionary in a remote village in a country in Africa. But she had contracted malaria and was in a terrible condition. There was no nearby hospital and no road for a car to take her for treatment.

When the pastor was speaking in tongues, he was actually talking in the native language of those people in Africa where her daughter was based. The minister spoke or prophesied, "Mama, your daughter is healed from malaria right now, begin to thank God for the healing." She explained that her daughter used to teach her that native language when she would come home for a time. Everybody in the church was edified and began to thank God too. Tongues edify believers because they are loaded with the presence of God.

Praying in Tongues

We have shortly explained the slight difference between speaking and praying. We know speaking as noted earlier is declaring, advising or saying something to a person or a situation.

However, *praying* in tongues emphasizes the art of communication between the speaker and God but in tongues. When we are praying in tongues, the Holy Spirit within us is actually talking to the Father on our behalf or on behalf of others on certain matters. We can't understand unless interpreted. The Spirit of God acts like a lawyer representing a client for the reason that the client doesn't know his rights or lacks judiciary protocols. (Rom. 8:26-27)

For example, back in my home village in South Sudan, some missionaries from Germany were holding a revival meeting in one of our churches. They engaged the Christians to pray. One of the ladies, who could not read or write, was praying in tongues but in a foreign language. After finishing prayers, one of the missionaries approached her and began to talk to her in the German that lady was speaking. He said she was praying in a fluent German language, *revealing certain matters and asking God to intervene.* He began to unwrap the message to the people which amazed everyone.

How did that happen? It is beyond human understanding! Only the Spirit of God knows. Part two of this book will explain how we can hear God through our tongues to help us walk in the perfect will of God.

Paul simplifies for us that praying in tongues, like speaking in tongues, is spearheaded by the Holy Spirit and the human spirit not the mind. In other words, the Spirit of God engages our human spirit to make utterances in which the mind gains no understanding. Thus he says, "if I pray in an unknown tongue, my spirit prayeth, but my understanding is unfruitful." (1 Cor. 14:14)

So when you are praying in tongues and you may not understand what you are praying about, remember that in the realm of the spirit, you are helping to prevent others from being attacked by the devil, delivering people from demonic intrusions and declaring blessings upon people including yourself. Praying in tongues is awesome! That is why Paul advises churches to "forbid not to speak with tongues." (v.39)

Praying *with* the spirit and Praying *in* the Spirit

Several scriptures talk about praying with the *spirit* or praying in the *Spirit*. Let's be keen to understand that any scripture talking about spirit with lowercase "s" may refer to human spirit, gifting endowments (such as the spirit of wisdom) or demonic spirit if the context allows otherwise. But if the Spirit is written using uppercase "S" it refers to the Holy Spirit.

For example, Paul says in 1 Corinthians 14:15 that there are times he prays to God not using his mind or understanding but his spirit: "What is it then? *I will pray with the spirit*, and I will pray with the understanding also: I will sing with the spirit, and I will sing with the understanding also." (emphasis italicized) The "spirit" Paul is talking here is the spirit of man, not the Holy Spirit, even though some versions relate the Holy Spirit to it in parenthesis.

Some instances, however, the Bible talks about praying "in" the Spirit of God. "But ye, beloved, building up yourselves on your most holy faith, *praying in the Holy Ghost*." (Jude 1:20 emphasis italicized)

Remember the words "spirit" and "Spirit" are sometimes interchangeable, depending on which version you use. Our current Bible versions have been edited throughout history which has affected some important concepts thus confusing people to grasp the truth. We have to pray for God's insight.

Let's come back to praying "with" the spirit concept. When you pray with the spirit, you are engaging your own spirit to pray using the spirit's way of *utterance*. It may not necessarily mean you are praying "in" the Holy Spirit. The Holy Spirit usually catches the "engaged" spirit to catch the fire from within.

People who pray in tongues do not usually start in the Spirit of God. They engage their human spirit first and then an explosion happens as they *fervently* continue praying. That is why the Bible tells us that prophesying— of course including praying with the spirit or speaking in tongues—is under our control. (1 Cor. 14:32)

Paul reveals the secrets of his prayers. He says there are times he does both praying or singing: one with the spirit and the other one using his mind. This would help others say "amen." "What is it then? I will pray with the spirit, and I will pray with the understanding also: I will sing with the spirit, and I will sing with the understanding also." (v.15) Paul didn't stop Christians from praying in tongues in church. He only warns of speaking a message meant to the congregation in tongues and that it must be interpreted and must be done orderly. You cannot address me using a language I don't understand and then expect me to reply. It doesn't make sense.

I do interpret for preachers preaching in Arabic to English or the other languages that I know since God has blessed me with several languages. I am asked to interpret because some group in the audience don't understand the language the preacher uses. If it is not interpreted to them, they can't get it.

This is similar to tongues. Speaking and praying in tongues that is meant as prophecy needs interpretation to edify the church.

But some moments *I don't* interpret preachers' prayers unless their prayers are meant as prophecy to the audience.

CONVICTION OF UNBELIEVERS THROUGH TONGUES

When we were growing up, a European missionary doctor spoke to my elder brother using our mother tongue which astonished all of us. We had to find out how she knew our language. When she came to do the vaccinations in our village, all the kids became friendly with her and did not mind the pain of the injections. We found a sense of "belonging" and "acceptance" by a wider European community represented by that doctor simply because she used our mother tongue. We later found out that she took the effort to learn our language so that her medical endeavors and Gospel message would resonate among the community. The few words she was using in my mother tongue were "ice breakers" for the many things to come forth from her mouth—the Gospel message.

Speaking in tongues when done decently and interpreted with the conviction of God, will allow unbelievers to take an interest in the things of God and try to understand the promptings leading to those miraculous utterances—then salvation will begin.

I remember I was once in a neighboring country in Africa and if I wanted to communicate to people in that community, I would use English or their language that I knew a little. But one time I was in a public bus and was surprised to hear two guys sitting behind me conversing in my mother tongue. I paid attention to them. I didn't hesitate. I went and sat next to them and began to ask them where they came from and how they knew my language.

This was what attracted the worshippers at the day of Pentecost in Jerusalem. They were hearing the "drunk" people at the upper room speaking their own languages and dialects which caught their attention.

Peter stood to preach explaining everything that was going on and challenged them to believe in Jesus Christ to receive tongues. Who knows, they might have already been preached in their own mother tongues through the tongues spoken at the upper room! (Acts 2:11) It was easy for them to accept Jesus Christ as Lord and Savior because they had already received a supernatural proof.

Similarly, Paul explains that when we speak in tongues, it is a sign to unbelievers to see the omniscience and omnipotence of God. "Wherefore tongues are for a sign, not to them that believe, but to them that believe not: but prophesying serveth not for them that believe not, but for them which believe." (1 Cor. 14:22)

For example, if you speak in tongues using a language known to nonbelievers and they know you don't speak their language what do you think would come into their mind? They would want to investigate more as to how you know their language just like my quest in the bus or my village kids who embraced that European missionary. Your explanation of the Gospel to them would be fruitful.

Sid Roth, the founder of *It's Supernatural* once invited two Filipino couples to his house. The couple were medical practitioners—the husband was also a university professor of medicine. The wife was born again, but her husband was not, just a professing Roman Catholic.

At prayer time they all held hands together and Sid began to pray in tongues using a language unknown to him. After "amen" the professor asked Sid how he knew his own Filipino dialect. Sid was surprised and then asked him what he (Sid) was praying about. The professor said, "You prayed, 'You must repent of your sins and believe in the Messiah…'"

The professor was convicted of sin and was born again at that moment. Later, they, along with Sid, began to distribute salvation tracts on streets and schools. Is that not amazing?

Last night before writing this passage, Pr. Emmanuel Twagirimana originally from Rwanda was speaking in the church I attended. He died due to the shrapnel from a bomb that hit him during the 1994 Rwanda Genocide. A horrific event which killed around a million people in less than hundred days.

His dead body was wrapped in a blanket and taken to a room where many bodies were stored since no one was able to bury them. They started to decay.

When he died, he was taken to heaven and shown many amazing things. After seven days in heaven, he came back to life. He narrated that in heaven he met Jesus and was told to come back to earth to preach the Gospel worldwide. Jesus also handed him a Bible to eat and assured him that since he spoke only his native language he was not to worry about languages.

One time he went to Sweden with his interpreter to preach for three days. God used him mightily and many people came to the Lord. But the night before the last day, his interpreter disappeared into the city refusing to go back to Rwanda. The following morning when his host pastor came to pick them up, his interpreter was nowhere to be found.

He could only communicate with the host pastor using sign language. They went to the revival meeting and the auditorium was filled with people. He began to pray for God to give him a Swedish tongue to be able to speak to the people. He reminded God of the promises Jesus assured him not to worry about languages and after seeking God he gained some peace.

When he came to the podium to speak, he began by praying in tongues and realized he was speaking Swedish.

All the people in the gathering went wild. Thousands accepted Jesus Christ as Lord and Savior and many got healed.

Instead of three days in Sweden, he remained there for three months—speaking Swedish fluently.

After his testimony spread, a Rwandan student doctor studying in Sweden came to visit him. The moment they began to talk in Kinyarwanda, the tongue language (Swedish) disappeared. From thereon that lady became his interpreter the rest of his days there.

This amazing testimony seems beyond comprehension. It was videotaped.

Pr. Emmanuel met the Pope, several presidents and Queen Elizabeth of England where he prayed for her. Pastor Emmanuel wrote a book: *7 Days in Heaven.*

Tongues create avenues for the Gospel to find a space in the hearts of nonbelievers.

CHAPTER 2

TONGUES BYPASS THE MIND

Speaking in tongues is puzzling to the human mind. The mind finds it difficult to comprehend. To many, speaking in tongues looks funny, laughable and nonsense. To others, tongues are regarded as tenets of faith for certain denominations. So if you are not a member of those denominations, you are "excused" from speaking in tongues.

Imagine that you are in a room packed with a lot of people and everyone there begins to randomly speak in different languages to catch your attention. You hear them speak in your mother tongue and in other languages you do not know. You might conclude that there is something unusual going on with those speaking. You will even question yourself if really those speaking, shouting and yelling are healthy in their mind.

The same trend happened on the day of Pentecost. The people who came to Jerusalem to worship God rushed to the "babbling" scene to ascertain the happening with those at the upper room. They were amazed and got confused: "And they were all amazed, and were in doubt, saying one to another, What meaneth this? Others mocking said, These men are full of new wine." (Acts 2:12-13)

Such confusion and mind dilemma compelled Peter to make an exegesis so that the onlookers might get saved and grasp the anointing of tongues. His detailed sermon convicted over three thousand souls to accept Jesus Christ as Lord and Saviour. (v.41-42)

Even today, speaking in tongues is still causing great misunderstanding in churches. Different charismatic movements have broken out from mainstream churches and formed new denominations—they claim the baptism of the Holy Spirit, which enables one to speak in tongues, is purposely muted by mainstream churches.

On the other hand, those who are not filled in the Holy Spirit look at tongues as "devilish" or utterances that are "coined" by cunning Christians just for whatever reasons. Even many of the believers speaking in tongues have no idea what they are speaking. They just know some "urge" within them is influencing them to utter mysteries and yet they have no clue of how to decode those mysteries.

Some of them just enjoy the "vibes" coming from their mouths and the electric-like current flowing within them. They don't know that they are making promulgations, declarations, intercession, commanding in a mysterious language. You have to know, as I quoted Paul earlier: "anyone who speaks in a tongue does not speak to people but to God. Indeed, no one understands them; they utter mysteries by the Spirit."

The Apostle Paul knew speaking in tongues avoids the mind because of its carnality. He knew tongues could be abused by the mind and that is why the mind looks at it as a mystery. No one understands unless there is a divine help to interpret and the interpretation comes from the Spirit too. The mind can't comprehend divine matters.

Recent medical research in the US has found that speaking in tongues is truly supernatural. It bypasses the human mind as claimed by tongues speakers and clearly reiterated in 1 Corinthians 14:14: "For if I pray in an unknown tongue, my spirit prayeth, but my understanding is unfruitful."

Dr. Andrew Newman from the University of Pennsylvania, who spearheaded this medical finding, asserts that when humans speak, the activity takes place in the part of their brain called *frontal lobe*.

He first researched Franciscan nuns and Buddhists who devote themselves to continual praying. Their frontal lobes were found *busy*—meaning they use their mind to formulate words in prayers.

Dr. Andrew then examined some pastors and ministers who claim to be filled in the Holy Spirit with the ability to speak in tongues. Each one was asked to pray with understanding using their mind while being x-rayed. Their frontal lobes exhibited a lot of activity just like the nuns and Buddhists.

After that, Dr. Andrew asked each one again to speak in the supernatural language while being x-rayed. Here come the astonishing results: their frontal lobes exhibited *no activity*.

The research concluded that the supernatural prayer language or speaking in tongues emanates from a different source other than the mind—Christians call that "source" the spirit.

We can assuredly say the supernatural prayers come from within the human spirit not the mind: "if I pray in an unknown tongue, *my spirit prayeth*, but my understanding is unfruitful."

WEAKNESS OF MIND IN KNOWING

Let's imagine that two of you are to stand before a judge in a court. You, however, decide to be on your own and speak for yourself before the judge. But the other person hired a renowned lawyer to speak on his behalf. Who do you think would win the case? The answer is obvious. The person hiring a lawyer will definitely win the case and the probability of you losing is quite high.

The reason you would lose the court case is that you are not trained in things to do with the law of the land and in particular to the rights and procedures pertaining your care. You don't even know the judiciary protocols.

The other person will win the case because he hired a lawyer who knows his rights and the judiciary system.

Similarly, the Holy Spirit does such advocacy. He is sent by the Father to help us in our prayers and intercession. He comes from the throne of God and knows every procedure and protocol.

But before going deeper, we need to know exactly the place from where tongues emanate. Are they scattered all over the body or centered in the human spirit? If so, then where is the human spirit located? Is it within the heart, the belly or somewhere near the mind? As we go deep in learning about the spirit world, try to position yourself ready to receive something from God as you continue reading.

Situation Room for Tongues

In my other book "Power" I explained the composition of humans in detail as revealed in the Bible. But here we will briefly touch on the three components that describe humans. Paul prays, "May your whole *spirit, soul* and *body* be kept blameless at the coming of our Lord Jesus Christ." (1 Thes. 5:23 emphasis italicized)

The physical feature of human is the body which we can see and touch. The invisible feature of the body is the soul housing emotions, will and mind. It cannot be seen or touched, but its reactions impact the body. The human spirit is the *core* that differentiates us from animals. It is where we have the sense of worship and the feeling of guilt. It's the "meeting place" between humanity and divinity. In other words, it's where human spirit meets with Holy Spirit. We might call it the "control room" controlling our lives.

When Adam sinned, the glorious Spirit of God distanced Himself from the human spirit and the human spirit becomes unresponsive to God thus awaiting damnation. (Rom. 3:23; 5:12) When a person gets born again the Spirit of God comes to meet the human spirit and regenerates it to live. The Holy Spirit then becomes a permanent resident in the person. The body becomes His house but has to be kept clean. "Surely you know that you are God's temple and that God's Spirit lives in you! God will destroy anyone who destroys God's temple. For God's temple is holy, and you yourselves are his temple." (1 Cor. 3:16-17 NLT)

When you are born again and filled in the Spirit where you can utter mysteries, the utterance emanates from the Holy Spirit who resides within you.

Once you are filled with the Holy Ghost, you can sense some movement within you as well as vocalization. People often report electric-like currents moving all over their body. Internally a lot of "unusual" reactions are felt, and the urge for prayer is evidenced. When you start praying, you find yourself uttering statements unintended by your mind. It's the Spirit avoiding the mind to declare heavenly statements.

Jesus knew how important it is to be filled in the Spirit. He encouraged His disciples not to worry that He would leave them orphans. He promised to send a

Helper to advocate for them. The Advocate comes from the Father and knows exactly how to approach the throne of Grace when making petitions. "But the Advocate, the Holy Spirit, whom the Father will send in my name, will teach you all things and will remind you of everything I have said to you." (John 14:26 NIV)

When He came upon the disciples on Pentecost day, tremendous ministerial success was realized. "Then they that gladly received his word were baptized: and the same day there were added unto them about three thousand souls." (Acts 2:41)

It was not the fashion of their words that convicted the onlookers; it was the power of the Holy Spirit.

Traffic Jams in the Mind

Speaking in tongues bypasses the weak mind of humans. Romans 8:26, 27 clearly reveals to us the power of praying in the Spirit and weakness of the mind: "In the same way, the Spirit helps us in our weakness. We do not know what we ought to pray for, but the Spirit himself intercedes for us through wordless groans. And he who searches our hearts knows the mind of the Spirit, because the Spirit intercedes for God's people by the will of God."

When you are filled with the Holy Spirit and speak in tongues it is not your mind speaking, it is the Spirit of God speaking through you. The Spirit is speaking things that are beneficial to your life and others.

King James Version accuses the mind of "infirmity." It is distorted with human inadequacies—depression, stress, confusion and many abnormalities.

The human mind is every time bombarded with regrets of the past, bills to pay, debts and problems thus making it weak to interact with God.

In the city where I live, there is a bypass road adjacent to the downtown. The bypass is wide with many lanes and is used for speedy driving and long destinations. The posted speed is almost double the normal speed inside the downtown. It has only few traffic lights but in its favor— always green.

Within the downtown, heavy traffic jams are always evidenced. If two people compare trips where one drives through the downtown and the other along the bypass to a distant destination, guess who will reach the destination first? The one using the bypass will reach it first and the other one will be caught up in heavy traffic and be stopped numerous times.

Speaking in tongues is like using a bypass road.

It avoids the mind and all kind of mind activity that hinders prayers. What you are transmitting from your inner man goes direct to the Father for deliberation. The "traffic jam" in our mind makes it difficult to analyze events and filter words.

Probably many Spirit-filled believers don't exercise the gift of tongues daily because they have no idea how important tongues are for them. Others misuse, abuse and relegate tongues because of ignorance in understanding the secret behind tongues. That is why the Bible says in Matthew 7:6 that, "Give not that which is holy unto the dogs, neither cast ye your pearls before swine, lest they trample them under their feet, and turn again and rend you."

Let's not make God regret why He gave us holy gifts when we keep trampling or relegating them.

WEAKNESS OF MIND IN PRAYING

Praying with our mind has certain deficiencies. Romans 8:26 reveals that, in most cases, we even don't know the actual needs to ask from God. "For we know not what we should pray for as we ought: but the Spirit itself maketh intercession for us with groanings which cannot be uttered."

We pray according to our human understanding and make requests in accordance with what we see necessary to us. But when we allow the Spirit of God to pray for us, He knows our actual needs and the intentions of God towards us as individuals. He will then plead before the throne of Grace for the Father to answer us. "And he that searcheth the hearts knoweth what is the mind of the Spirit, because he maketh intercession for the saints according to the will of God." (v.27)

My elder brothers used to request me to ask our father to grant them certain requests. They knew our father was very close to me. Any time they needed something they would tell me and I would then ask my father. In most cases our father would grant what was requested because he didn't have doubts about me—he trusted me. But if my brothers would go to ask him directly, he would have a lot of questions.

Remember how, when Jesus predicted that one of the disciples was going to betray Him all the twelve were confused. Instead they asked John to ask Jesus. They knew John was close to Jesus. So Jesus was able to reveal the person who was going to betray Him only to John. "Then the disciples looked one on another, doubting of whom he spake. Now there was leaning on Jesus' bosom one of his disciples, whom Jesus loved. Simon Peter, therefore beckoned to him, that he should ask who it should be of whom he spake. He then lying on Jesus' breast saith unto him, Lord, who is it? Jesus answered, He it is, to whom I shall give a sop, when I have dipped it. And when he had dipped the sop, he gave it to Judas Iscariot, the son of Simon." (John 13:22-26)

The Apostle John knew deep secrets of Jesus Christ because of his closeness with the Lord. That could be also one of the reasons he was entrusted to write the closing eschatological book of the Bible summing up detailed plans of God for the future and the formation of new heavens and new earth.

Similarly, and so uniquely, when compared to Apostle John, the Spirit of God in us knows the exact mind of God because He came from the Father and is God Himself. When you pray in tongues, you allow the Holy Spirit in you to intercede before the Father on your behalf.

Limits of Mind in Articulation

The other importance of praying in tongues is that the Spirit helps grab words that are exactly pertinent to your request. The mind can become weak and lack expression because it operates naturally. That is why Jesus confirms in Matthew 26:41 that when praying "the spirit indeed is willing, but the flesh is weak."

Just imagine that you come from work and you are tired, but you want to start praying. You will definitely lack words to express yourself. Some may even start yawning and say words that are horrible. What if you have been "yelled" at by your boss at work or you are quarreling with your children? Starting to pray is very hard. Your conscience has already condemned you of dishonesty. So your prayers won't seem successful.

Sometimes many Christians hold grudges in their hearts without forgiving the people who caused them. The moment you start praying with a grudge in your heart, the focus shifts. The images of those who have wronged you begins to surface. What do you think could be the result of your prayers? Nothing! But when you begin to pray in tongues the Spirit of God starts convicting you and allowing you to release whoever has wronged you.

Rescue through Tongues

Tongues can save your life and the life of others.

One time I drove several women by car from the city of Vancouver to Calgary, Alberta, for a revival meeting. The journey took 12 hours. We passed through the Rocky Mountains of North America. As we were driving, the Spirit of God alerted me of a forthcoming accident on the way.

To my surprise, one of the women sitting behind me started speaking vigorously in tongues. The others followed. I immediately knew God through their prayers was preventing something terrible from happening to us. I drove carefully.

Less than ten minutes later, in a narrow, sloppy corner I saw several cars overturned and totally blocking the road. A big truck had slid and the following car had crashed into the big truck followed by several other cars. I managed to stop in time. It was a rescue from above. The tongues helped us indeed. So if tongues are as important as we have just narrated, what prevents you from receiving or exercising them daily?

Because we often use our mind in prayers, many dilute their prayers with *begging*. They take hours begging God to intervene in their situations. Prayer is not meant for begging; it is meant for communion with

God. Those who believe in the Lord are no longer outcasts, but kings. Jesus "hath made us kings and priests unto God and his Father; to him be glory and dominion for ever and ever." (Rev.1:6) If so, then why do you beg God?

Do you think kings beg? No! They declare things. They use commands because they know their status in the kingdom. You never know, when you speak in tongues, you maybe declaring, decreeing and commanding certain things.

Allow the Advocate to speak on your behalf before the throne of Grace. Your mind is not keen enough to comprehend heavenly protocols. But the Spirit of God does, since He is God Himself who was sent to help us. (John 16:7)

WEAKNESS OF MIND IN REMEMBERING

Are you able to remember everything you did yesterday—the people whom you met, the words you used in your conversations? If you went to church last Sunday can you remember everything in the preaching?

Jesus had spent over three years with the disciples, taught them and revealed great mysteries about life matters but they barely remembered them.

Sometimes they would ask questions that had already been revealed to them. They didn't recognize who Jesus was even though He revealed Himself to them. That made Him wonder about their belief and memory: 'Jesus said, "For a long time I have been with you all; yet you do not know me, Philip?"' (John 14:9 GNT)

Due to memory deficiency of humans the Father resolved to send a "backup memory" to resolve those memory issues. "But the *Comforter*, which is the Holy Ghost, whom the Father will send in my name, he shall teach you all things, and *bring all things to your remembrance*, whatsoever I have said unto you." (v.26 emphasis italicized)

Even though you are a good driver, when you drive for long hours you become tired and barely attune to traffic alerts. That is why drivers often buy coffee or whatever necessary to keep them awake to avoid accidents. Don't trust your mind to comprehend everything, especially divine matters. You need help from above—you need the Holy Spirit.

Memory Storage Limit

Have you ever dreamt in a night but after waking up you find yourself not remembering the dream? You may know you had a dream, but you can't remember it.

We are reminded that God also gives messages, instructions and opportunities to us using dreams. (Num. 12:6) So if you keep forgetting, how can you walk circumspectly as per the instructions revealed in your dream?

Sometimes when you plan to pray for certain issues if you don't organize yourself properly by writing the requests, petitions down you may forget important areas to pray about. This not only happens while praying, but also while memorizing Bible verses.

I have been asked by many believers to pray for them. Generally, they say they keep forgetting important Bible verses they tried to memorize. Others blame the devil for blurring their memories.

Your limited memory needs a supernatural boost to store scriptures. Exercise your spirit through tongues to boost your memory. This can initially and continuously be done by allowing the Word of God to scan your mind, delete any unwanted files and remove dangerous viruses to make it conform to heavenly norms. (Rom. 12:2)

Thus Paul says, "if I pray in an unknown tongue, my

spirit prayeth, but my understanding is unfruitful." (1 Cor. 14:14) Here the expression "my understanding is unfruitful" is telling us that praying in tongues does not originate from the mind. It comes right from the human spirit spearheaded by the Holy Ghost. Such prayer avoids the mind for its weakness and limit in dealing with divine matters.

The Bible has already diagnosed the limitation of human mind with memory disease that needs divine intervention: "Likewise the Spirit also helpeth our infirmities: for we know not what we should pray for as we ought: but the Spirit itself maketh intercession for us with groanings which cannot be uttered." (Rom. 8:26)

Here one of the "infirmities" Paul alludes to our mind is *memory limit*. The best solution to revitalize it is by boosting it through the Word and providing a data storage in the spirit. When we pray in tongues, the Holy Spirit is able to retrieve those stored messages from the database for deliberation.

Memory Storage Aid

In one way or another, the Holy Spirit in terms of prayer acts as a memory aid to believers. Remember during the Pentecost day preaching in Acts, Peter did a fantastic job. He gave a detailed proof about Jesus

Christ, revealing Old Testament verses spoken about Jesus by King David, His vicarious death on the Cross, His glorious triumph and the outpouring of the Holy Spirit. The detailed truth Peter expounded in this sermon brought three thousand people on their knees to turn to Jesus Christ for salvation.

How did he remember all these? It was not his wisdom at all; they received a fresh memory to help them understand detailed matters of the kingdom.

What about Evangelist Stephen! How did he remember all the details he narrated to those ready to attack him because of his faith in Jesus Christ? For most of us it would have been a time to shiver—he was in a critical spot— facing looming mob justice. But instead 'Stephen was filled with the Holy Spirit. He looked toward heaven, where he saw our glorious God and Jesus standing at his right side. Then Stephen said, "I see heaven open and the Son of Man standing at the right side of God!"' (Acts 7:55-56 CEV)

Jesus was with the disciples for three and a half years teaching them the kingdom. The Bible never told us that they wrote, copied or recorded the words of Jesus. They instead listened to Him and sometimes asked Jesus to clarify for them difficult lessons and yet they forgot. When Jesus rose from the dead, they couldn't believe. (John 20:2, 9) Thomas wanted to touch His wounds first. (v.25)

However, when the Holy Spirit was sent, they began to remember all that Jesus told them and then handed us the detailed mission of Jesus Christ through the Gospel. What an amazing work of the Holy Spirit superseding the mind in memory and all sorts of functionalities.

Note the writing of scriptures! If you read other religious books such as the Quran, you find very contradictory statements—one opposing the other. But the Bible was written over a period of approximately 1,500 years and yet each book supports and interprets one another. It's the memory of the Spirit filling pious men to write.

"All scripture is given by inspiration of God, and is profitable for doctrine, for reproof, for correction, for instruction in righteousness: That the man of God may be perfect, thoroughly furnished unto all good works." (2 Tim. 3:16-17) "For the prophecy came not in old time by the will of man: but holy men of God spake as they were moved by the Holy Ghost." (2 Pet. 1:21)

CHAPTER 3

TONGUES BYPASS SATAN

The country of South Sudan had been at war with the then Government of the Sudan for over 55 year from just days before the Independence of the Sudan in 1956 (after the Condominium Rule involving Britain and Egypt). Several rebellions, coup d'états and forced Islamization took place which cost over two and one-half million lives. South Sudan ceded from the rest of the Sudan in 2011 in a referendum election.

When Britain was leaving, she handed the Government into the hands of the elite Arabs in the northern Sudan and asked them to share with the southerners. But the following day after the declaration of independence, actions were reversed—the Government was made up of only northerners—in fact Arabs themselves—with exception of a few members of parliament from the southern region. Forced Islamization was enacted into the Constitution even though the south was predominately Christians and animists.

War broke out (1955-1972) led by prominent southerners such as General Emilio Tafeng, Ali Gbattala, Fr. Saturnino Lohure, Aggrey Jaden, General Joseph Lagu among others. The Movement was known as the *Anya Nya,* which loosely translates to "snake venom." Later, a peace agreement was signed in Addis Ababa, Ethiopia.

A short time later the peace agreement was abrogated and Sharia was passed into law. Economic deprivation of the south began surfacing and rampant killing of southern professionals continued with impunity. In 1983 Dr. John Garang from the south rebelled when he was sent to annihilate internal rebellions within the Government army in Bor town, a southern part of the Sudan. Dr. John Garang formed a gallant rebellion force in the south named Sudan People's Liberation Army/Movement (SPLA/SPLM) which became a "thorn in the flesh" to the central Government in Khartoum, Sudan.

The SPLA of the south captured many strategic places in southern Sudan and advanced to capture many towns in the north which forced the Khartoum government to sign a Comprehensive Peace Agreement (CPA) in 2005 with President Omar Hassan al-Bashir. This allowed two separate Government armies—the SPLA overseeing the south while Sudan Armed Forces (SAF) overseeing the northern part of the Sudan.

Before Omar Hassan al-Bashir became a president in a coup d'état in 1989, he commanded the Government forces in the eastern Equatoria region of southern Sudan based in Torit town. Omar Al-Bahir had a very hard time fighting with a certain rebel commander who almost captured him several times.

After signing the peace agreement, it was widely reported that President Omar al-Bashir asked Dr. John Garang to send to him that "stubborn" rebel commander so that he would pay homage to him.

When they met we are told President Omar al-Bashir hugged him, made a statement in Arabic: *Inta rajul hagiga*—meaning "you are indeed a gentleman" typifying his braveness in fighting wars with diligence.

That military commander, currently a top government official in South Sudan, used to devise unpredictable strategies and in most cases would win the battles.

When he wanted to attack a military base he would map out the base on paper, identify strategic areas and draw plans to launch his attacks. On a daily basis he would create coded messages for his junior officers making them difficult to be understood by outsiders. The purpose was to avoid leaking information to the enemy and also prevent tapping of communications. The enemy would only hear a "gibberish" sound but had no idea what it was about or its meaning. They would only realize a sudden attack.

Even today this commander is a well-respected top government official in the Republic of South Sudan and works in top strategic areas in the national security.

You have to understand that our enemy watches over believers' movements, plans and fellowships. He wants to hear everything so that he can frustrate us, even kill us. If you always reveal your plans to him through conscious praying, the enemy may learn your thoughts and work against you. Code your praying through tongues to bypass his understanding to catch him off guard.

CRAFTINESS OF SATAN AGAINST BELIEVERS

When you accept Jesus Christ as Lord and Savior, satan sees you as a rebel who has broken away from his kingdom. He will plan all kinds of ways to bring you back under his control. He may use different strategies to lure you back to him but be on your guard always and pray with all kinds of prayers and more so, in tongues.

Some of satan's craftiness may look similar to what we think as God's. He would speak messages that resemble God's. See the case of Paul and Silas in Acts 16:16-17. The spirit of divination in the girl was commending the work of Paul to be godly. This demonic spirit even encouraged people to listen to these men of God. The spirit was just using tricks to divert the work of God.

Just like Paul, we need to develop our discernment to recognize the tactics of satan. He may come as sheep but he is very harmful to believers. "Beware of false prophets, which come to you in sheep's clothing, but inwardly they are ravening wolves." (Matt. 7:15)

Exercise your tongues to frustrate satan with his evil plans against your life, family or ministry.

Monitoring Spirits against Believers

The Apostle Paul, Prophet Silas (including Pastor Timothy and Dr. Luke) were in Philippi witnessing Jesus Christ to many. As they went around, a slave girl possessed with the spirit of divination was monitoring them and advertising their mission of salvation asking sinners to listen to these men who were bringing good news to them. She went on and on until Paul and his team were perturbed. He rebuked the monitoring spirit in the girl to leave and he left at once. (Acts 16:18)

The monitoring spirit spoke facts about Paul and the team and yet he is evil: "These men are servants of the Most High God! They announce to you how you can be saved." (v.17 GNT) How did the evil spirit know that Paul and Silas were ministers of the Word?

On the other hand, we learned that this slave girl was used by her masters for profit. She would precisely predict things to those coming for consultation. The spirits of divination are monitoring spirits; they monitor the movement of people and leak all their information which would be used for prediction but with evil intent.

The air around us is contaminated with evil forces that listen to people's conversation and then use this information against them. Any word that we speak into the air can easily be caught by evil powers. That is why Paul emphasizes that our actual war is not physical but spiritual. We fight principalities in the air. (Eph. 6:12) They are there monitoring and watching what people do.

For this reason, the Bible advises us to control our tongues—the way we speak. "Keep thy tongue from evil, and thy lips from speaking guile." (Ps. 34:13) If we curse or utter profanities, the monitoring spirits hear and then use our words to cause havoc.

Likewise, so many prayers of Christians who only prefer praying with the mind have been leaked by monitoring spirits and have devised ways to thwart the intended outcomes.

The earnest prayer of Prophet Daniel was hacked by satan. The monitoring spirits roaming in the air heard everything Daniel channeled to God. They blocked the reply until Archangel Michael came to clear the way. (Dan. 10:1-13)

If Daniel were to speak in tongues, his prayers would bypass the devil. Of course no one in the Old Testament was speaking in tongues since the Holy Spirit was not yet poured out as on the day of Pentecost.

Those who fear God in the Old Testament had a hard time praying. The enemy was frequently hacking their prayers to twist things around. The only thing that helped them was to clothe themselves by abiding under the shadow of the Almighty for coverage. (Ps. 119:1)

But today we are lucky. When you are filled with the Holy Spirit and speak in tongues, your tongues frustrate satan. He cannot know what you are telling God. As you pray in the Spirit, God will also render you "flushes" of the happenings in the spirit realms including the satanic plans. What an amazing God we serve!

Tongues use codes unknown to satan and his monitoring agents. They would hear the sound babbling but have no idea about their meaning. The words in tongues bypass satan's comprehension thus making him weak and useless.

Ploy of satan against Believers

The Bible tells us that Paul was monitored in his move in Philippi and the evil spirit kept announcing their mission until he was annoyed. (Acts 16:18)

What do you think could be the aim of this monitoring spirit following Paul? He was there to frustrate Paul to get him to deviate from the truth. In fact, Paul became "grieved" as we read. The focus on the gospel was sliding to something else—*flesh*. But Paul was very discerning and he acted quickly before things went off track. He knew it was the devil disguising himself to talk the truth. He had to command him out of the girl and satan did come out.

Elijah prayed for God to open the eyes of his servant so that he could see the angelic army supporting them. (2 Kings 6:17) Also note that there was a multitude of demonic forces by the side of the Syrian army coming to capture Elijah for revealing their evil plans against the king of Israel.

Elijah assured his servant to "Fear not: for they that be with us *[the angelic army supporting them]* are more than they that be with them *[the demonic forces supporting the captors].*" (v.16 emphasis added) Paul tells us in Ephesians 6 that our war is spiritual indeed.

When you face failures in life, frustrations in ministry and other noble endeavors, you need to be aware there are some "impediments" happening in the realm of the spirit— you are being monitored. The devil is possibly behind your failures. He doesn't want you to succeed. Thwart his plans through tongues and commands. Save your life before it's too late! You have the authority in your mouth.

For example, we often hear reports of distractions in churches, especially during preaching where children start crying, running around and strange thoughts begin to occupy people's mind. The devil knows the message is going to change people's hearts for the better. He will devise ways to influence some children or older people to disrupt the message so that we perish for lack of faith through hearing the Word. "So then faith *comes* by hearing, and hearing by the word of God." (Rom. 10:17 NKJV)

A man once wanted to hear what God was saying to him through scriptures. He closed his eyes, randomly opened a page and put his finger on a verse. He found Matthew 27:5 saying Judas Iscariot "went and hanged himself." He closed the Bible again and opened another page. He put his finger on a second verse (Luke 10:37) and it reads "go and do likewise." He believed it was God telling him to die. He went and hanged himself.

That is exactly the ploy of the devil. He guided that man's finger to these verses where a meaning was retrieved out of context for the purpose of murder—and it happened. Imagine a believer doing that! Be on your guard and pray in tongues.

On the other hand, don't be a negative confessor. When you keep confessing negativities *into* yourself or your children, the negatives will come back in the form of misfortune. If you keep confessing poverty, the spirit of poverty will come to you. If you keep confessing fear, the spirit of fear will be sent to you by satan. Don't you know that "the tongue is a fire, a world of iniquity: so is the tongue among our members, that it defileth the whole body, and setteth on fire the course of nature; and it is set on fire of hell?" (James 3:6)

Today many people report seeing dead people appearing to them physically or in dreams. These dead people tell them to do certain rituals or incantations. This is not only happening in Asia or Africa but also in all the other continents. Is it true that your loved ones who have died, can have their spirits come back to you? No! It is the disguise of satan. The familiar spirits following them when they were alive are the ones disguising themselves in the form of humans just to confuse you.

Jesus gave us the understanding in the story of Lazarus and the rich man. The story reveals that once a person dies, his spirit cannot come back. If he did well before God, he will go to be with the Lord but if he didn't receive Christ as Lord and Savior, his spirit is sent to a place of torment and gnashing of teeth. (Matt. 25:46)

Bypass the craftiness of satan using sophisticated weapons—tongues utterance—to distance yourself from monitoring spirits and also abide in God's manifest presence.

DEFEAT OF SATAN THROUGH TONGUES

The Bible puts it clearly that to wage war against satan we have to go into the spirit realm and come out with enough authority and power to wreak havoc on the devil. If we just think humanly that we can defeat satan, this will backfire on us terribly. The sons of Sceva from the priestly lineage were badly hurt by devils after provoking them—intending to cast them out the way Paul did. (Acts 19:13-15) They thought Paul "just" spoke the words naturally without knowing that, the Apostle saturated his words with the power of the Holy Ghost thus causing terror to the enemy.

When you frequently speak in tongues, you will defeat the archenemy who follows you at all times. But it's not just a matter of speaking in tongues; you have to be in union with God.

Jesus encourages His disciples to be united with Him and remain in Him so that they would be protected and endowed with supernatural power to break bondages and invite blessings. "I am the vine, ye are the branches: He that abideth in me, and I in him, the same bringeth forth much fruit: for without me ye can do nothing." (John 15:5)

The enemy who prowls day and night to hurt us has been constitutionally defeated on the Cross by Jesus and the enemy has no rights to cling to you unless you otherwise invite him or live a reckless life devoid of *exousia* and *dunamis*.

We have all gone through spiritual recklessness in one way or the other. It could be due to ignorance—lack of spiritual knowledge—or purposeful inclination to wicked practices. Satan will get his rights from there to challenge us. But the enemy was disarmed on the Cross; he is trying to lure people away from God so that they would perish along with him in hell. Don't allow him to take advantage of you. Kick him out of your life.

Just a few weeks ago, the Spirit of the Lord led me to pray vigorously at my house with all kinds of prayers. I began to declare freedom around the area of my residence—attacking any evil forces assigned.

Shortly after prayers, I heard a burst—a "giant man" came in and furiously began to yell at me with frustration and indignation. He claimed I was destroying the foundations of their houses in the area every day with my prayers. They requested me not to pray "such kinds" of prayers—he meant tongues.

When I woke up, I realized it was a dream. I then knew tongues did wreak great havoc on satan who claimed to be the "real" property owner of the area.

Tongues are important to defeat any evil plan against our lives without us knowing what is being planned at the "locker room" by satan.

A woman on her way to a prayer meeting was prompted by the Spirit of the Lord to speak in tongues which attracted many onlookers. She had no idea what she was praying about. But later when she came home she realized thieves had broken into her house, pulled the drawer which contained some gold and cash. Tongues blindfolded their eyes—they could not see the valuables. In fact, they stole nothing in the house. Immediately that woman realized it was God who prompted her to defeat the evil plans against the family by speaking in tongues.

When Jesus revealed His mission of redemption to save the world through death, Peter refused to accept it. He did not want Jesus to redeem mankind. Instead of rebuking Peter who audibly spoke, Jesus rebuked satan behind Peter. He knew satan was using one of His closest allies to frustrate His way of salvation. "Get thee behind me, Satan: thou art an offense unto me: for thou savourest not the things that be of God, but those that be of men." (Matt. 16:23)

Still, satan's influence on Peter endured up to the arrest of Jesus. Peter took it as a physical fight as quoted in John 18:10 (ERV): "Simon Peter had a sword, which he pulled out. He struck the servant of the high priest and cut off his right ear. (The servant's name was Malchus.)"

What did Jesus do? He stopped Peter from the physical fight and told him "Put your sword back in its place! I must drink from the cup the Father has given me." (v.11) Jesus immediately performed a supernatural miracle and stitched the ear of the guard back on his head.

Any normal person seeing Jesus performing such miracles on the ear of Malchus would not even dare to draw near to arrest Him. They would be terrified and take off. Their clubs and power are nothing to Jesus. But yet they arrested Jesus and dragged Him away for questioning, beatings and then crucifixion. What made that resiliency in their hearts to have the guts to arrest Jesus? It was not them, but satan himself.

Satan thought Jesus would disobey the Father due to the pain of death. He believed he would triumph over Jesus the way he triumphed over Adam. But the second Adam was different. Instead, Jesus triumphed over satan and defeated death.

When you plan to serve the Lord in any area and your conscience testifies of its ingenuity to be noble, do it. But if you find a lot of resistance from the "Peters" take note that some invisible being is behind' them, planning to frustrate your good service. Remove that invisible person out of your way. Declare words and speak to your situation in tongues until peace emanates, proving the invisible enemy is scattered.

One of the world's renown, God's Generals, Dr. Oral Roberts, understood how speaking in tongues helped him survive. He told of an incident where he was invited to speak in a revival meeting organized by a friend for the first time.

Before he came to the podium, Dr. Roberts prayed in tongues declaring protection. As he was preaching someone with gun aimed and shot at his forehead but missed. He kept on preaching while the man was whisked away by police.

A few days later he visited that man in the prison to ask him why he wanted to kill him even though they didn't know each other. He got a shocking reply. The man confessed that "someone" was talking inside his mind to kill Oral Roberts. That "voice" inside him revealed that Oral Roberts was going to be a great asset to the kingdom of God. Unless Dr. Roberts was killed, their kingdom (satan's) would be scattered.

But guess what happened! Oral Roberts thought, "Oh I am going to be a great asset to God and my future is bright as such? Now I know."

Several headlines in the US newspapers read: "Young Evangelist shot amiss." That incident introduced him to the world and he began to receive invitations to preach from all over US and Europe.

Tongues frustrated satan and turned things better for the good of those who love the Lord. The teachers of the law had evil plans against Jesus. They did their best to stop the advancement of the message of Jesus about the kingdom. When Peter and John applied the name of Jesus to heal the crippled man at the entrance to the temple, the religious leaders were shaken. They arrested Peter and John, flogged them and warned them not to speak that name again. (Acts 4:18)

Instead, after Peter and John were released, they went back to their own fellowship and took part in the ongoing prayer meeting. They were filled with the Holy Spirit and preached boldly again. (v.31) Tongues can save us in situations where we experience intimidation.

Refill your glass with prayer every time.

PART II

DECODING TONGUES

CHAPTER 4

UNDERSTAND DIVERSE UTTERANCES

As humans, we may try to think we know details of spiritual matters especially when we have obtained "coveted" education degrees, have "accurately" prophesied occurrences which came to a pass, have prayed for healing and instant healings took place, and we speak in tongues more than others. Because of such myopic perceptions, any valuable idea we encounter which may be new or contradicting our stance is right away discarded.

The irony is that no one on earth can comprehend details of God and His special transactions with humanity. We only know a small part of His workings.

The disciples of Jesus wondered why Jesus was speaking figuratively to the outsiders but talking plainly to them. (Matt. 13:10) Yet they couldn't understand even though Jesus was talking plainly to them about the kingdom. They didn't understand until the Holy Spirit came to remind them what Jesus already explained as well as teach them new things, including tongues of course. (John 14:26)

Uttering diverse tongues are mysteries even still today. Many people think that tongues are only when a person speaks in a foreign language known by a certain group of people other than the speaker and therefore there is no other type of tongues other than that. But we also hear believers speaking in *gibberish* sounds—not a language spoken anywhere in the world and yet interpretations are given to that kind of babbling. What a mystery!

Paul prayed for the Ephesian brothers so that God would open their spiritual understanding to enable them know their divine calling. (Eph. 1:18) Paul knew from his spirit that many of these believers could not open their spiritual eyes and therefore they were stumbling around daily in life.

Understanding this book demands your openness of heart because it touches areas you probably have never thought about. Allow the Holy Spirit to speak to you as you go on reading so that you will be able to understand the various kinds of tongues we will tackle.

Decades ago, many traditional Christians viewed those who spoke in tongues as heretics and any Christian found speaking in tongues within their denominations would be excommunicated immediately.

But today, the controversy seems to be attenuating—for millions of Christians from the Roman Catholic, the Anglican, Methodist, Presbyterian, Baptist or Lutheran churches testify of baptism in the Holy Spirit with ability to speak in tongues as the Spirit gives them the utterance.

A few years ago, a renowned Baptist professor was asked by one of the Baptist Conventions in the United States to research the phenomenon of tongues speaking. This was done in order to prove its discrepancies so that no one within their denomination would dare to pursue tongues speaking, since many of their believers seeming attracted to the experience.

In three months, the professor did a thorough research work concerning the phenomenon of tongues. However, the trend went the other way—his finding convinced him that speaking in tongues is in fact biblical and still exists. It is meant to edify the church, bypass the human mind and confuse satan.

Three days before the beginning of the Convention,

he went into his closet to pray asking God to baptize him, if tongues really exist today. Surprisingly he was baptized and began to vigorously speak in tongues.

When he was asked to present his "academically" proven dissertation disqualifying the current trend of speaking in tongues, he went on to speak of his experience three days before the Convention began. He proved that tongues are real and even encouraged the Convention to seek for the gift instead.

He was immediately excommunicated and fired from his teaching career in one of the denomination's seminaries.

However, God opened new doors. He was accepted to teach in Oral Roberts University and appointed the dean of the school.

Speaking in tongues has diversities that we cannot comprehend unless God interprets it for us. The Bible reveals certain kinds of utterances that are angelic which cannot be attributed to any language on earth. (1 Cor. 13:1) In some instances, people who speak in tongues do speak foreign languages (*xenolalia*) that are spoken by other groups of people other than the speaker himself which amazes non-believers and convicts them for the Gospel. (Acts 2:1-12)

We will now differentiate speaking in *unknown* (gibberish) tongues from speaking in *other* (articulate) tongues as well as speaking wordless groans by the Spirit Himself which cannot be uttered and explained.

DYNAMICS OF SPEAKING GIBBERISH TONGUES

Over 400 years ago around 1611 A.D., the translators of King James Version (among other versions) added an italicized word "unknown" to identify the mysterious kind of the tongue Paul was trying to explain to the church of Corinth. (1 Cor. 14:2, 4, 13, 14) Many of them were already gibbering but chaotically. Other versions, however, use "a tongue" to underscore the common agreement denoting this mysterious utterance puzzling many. This kind of unknown tongue is not the tongues revealed in Acts 2:4-12 during the Pentecost day where the apostles were speaking articulate languages known by other nationalities.

The kind of speaking in tongues Paul states in Corinth is so gibberish—full of gobbledygook expressions. That is one of the major reasons it faces a lot of challenge from critics even today.

Speaking in asyllabic or gibberish tongues typifies utterance that is impossible to understand. The utterance sounds silly and yet Paul tells the church to "forbid not to speak with tongues." (1 Cor. 14: 39) He only gives certain guidelines on how to operate it especially during church worship when used in place of prophecy. (v.13, 26)

Gibberish Restructuring

God is spirit and by spirit law all spirit beings require physical bodies to use for physical manifestations. For example, when satan wants to manifests himself in nature, he possesses or influences people. That is why we see many demon-possessed people carry out evil plans. The evil spirit can sometimes be cast out from them—sometimes when they are allowed to speak they will confess where they come from and the reason for their possession.

On the other hand, during regeneration experience, God comes to live in the believer thus making his body His house. He uses the body to manifest His glory on earth but at the consent of the person.

So when we pray in tongues using silly vocalizations, the Spirit picks those unintelligent utterances to form excellent speeches in the spirit. If you gibber while praying, don't get upset if your utterances don't make sense. Yes, they don't make sense in the natural but in the spirit you utter articulate statements— well constructed.

Paul also says some of our tongue utterances are actually spoken by angels in heaven. (1 Cor.13:1) How expressive are the tongues of angels that men are able to speak? Was he exaggerating tongues because believers were forsaking love and minding only other spiritual gifts?

When you speak in unknown tongues, you may be speaking to your angels instructing them to execute certain works. That is interesting!

Dr. Oral Roberts once saw the Lord Jesus and also saw a tall angel standing beside himself. He asked the Lord who that person was. The Lord said it was his angel. At that time, Roberts was in need of finances to fulfill certain projects. The Lord said, "Talk to your angel." Immediately the angel said "send me." Then Roberts said "in the name of Jesus go" and he went and fulfilled the mission. Indeed, angels minister to us. (Heb. 1:14)

We have often heard believers who are filled in the power of the Holy Spirit enabling them to speak in tongues but using monosyllables. Others keep repeating certain consonants, vowels or words for long thus carrying meaningless connotation in the human perspective. But always keep in mind that God can pick any fizzy babbling and transcribe into a supernatural language.

However, there are certain Christians who claim they can speak in tongues but the reality is that they are not. They just mimic the tongues of other believers. Pray to God and ask Him to fill you. The utterance should be given by the Spirit not someone. "And they were all filled with the Holy Ghost, and [*the people*] began to speak with other tongues, as *the Spirit gave them utterance.*" (Acts 2:4 emphasis added)

If you speak in tongues don't be stagnant in speaking a certain way every time. Also be careful in mimicking others. I know of a believer who is Spirit-filled but when he hears a "renowned" minister speaking in tongues in a certain way, you will also hear him speaking same way. After he hears another person using a different version of tongues he will also speak that way. Can we call that plagiarism? That is fleshly and can hinder us from moving forward.

Interpreting unknown (gibberish) tongues is quite different from interpreting tongues spoken in articulate languages. The Pentecostal celebrants who were listening to the tongues of the Apostles at the upper room during the Pentecost day were able to understand what the apostles were speaking because they heard them speak in their own mother tongues. (v.6)

Actually the gibberish tongues need the Holy Spirit Himself to interpret meaning, thoughts or words inside the human spirit to be aired out. (1 Cor. 12:10)

One of the veteran charismatic ministers who spoke in tongues regularly and interpreted his own gibbering was Kenneth Hagin. He would sometimes groan and then interpret it himself or another person would stand to interpret. The power of God was vividly seen in his meetings.

Switching to Understanding

In the book of 1 Corinthians 14:15, Paul reveals his secret of victory that he often alters the way he prays and sings: "I will pray with the spirit, and I will pray with the understanding also: I will sing with the spirit, and I will sing with the understanding also." One reason which makes him switch his prayers and singing to understanding is to retrieve random statements whisked from his spirit.

When you come afresh from praying in tongues, start praying in your own language. You will find yourself speaking certain words that have not been planned by the mind. They just come randomly. If you take those statements into consideration, you will be amazed that God is talking to you, interpreting your tongues and answering your petitions.

Recently in a Sunday service, I was praying in tongues as well as praying with understanding. I spoke a full random statement about what God was doing at the service. I paused to think about the statement and I knew my mind hadn't manufactured those words.

Less than a minute later, another man from the congregation began to prophesy to the church. We all kept quiet. To my surprise, he repeated the exact statement I made when I switched from tongues to praying with understanding. I began to praise God for speaking through me as confirmed by that prophecy.

If I had prayed out loud, then one would think that person prophesying had heard me and did "plagiarize" my statements; but I was praying quietly to myself.

However, before you start praying, it is advisable to saturate your mind with the Word of God *first* to increase your faith. Find faith-building verses suiting your situation. Repeat speaking the words from the same verses until you are able to speak the words in memory without looking into your Bible.

Don't only end there, think about the words and their context. Check commentaries, concordance and root words in both Hebrews and Greek to link you to a wider understanding. Meditate on the words deeply until pictures from the context are building in your mind.

As you continue doing that, you will be building your faith into a level forcing you to begin praying. After honoring and thanking God start praying in tongues and then switch to an understandable language while declaring truth, power and commands into the areas of your need. If you feel the need to switch back to tongues, don't hesitate— alternate your praying until you are satisfied. Don't pray "nonstop" to only stop after amen.

After praying, spend a moment of quiet time just listening to your spirit. God will talk to you.

In understanding praying, the words coming from your mouth should not be attuned to begging but you should talk like a lawyer standing before a judge petitioning the court for consideration.

However, if you are praying to overturn negative situations, pray as if you are a judge rendering a verdict to a situation. You pray in that manner because you are under authority of Jesus and you use His name not your own "righteousness." I call this praying trend in my other published book entitled *Power* as "horizontal prayer direction—commanding praying." (p.131) This speaking praying is directed to an object or a situation. (Mark 11:23)

The moment we keep practicing such prayers, hearing God or sensing the movement of God in our lives becomes easy. God reveals His plans and words to people ready to receive Him and accept Him into their lives.

DYNAMICS OF SPEAKING ARTICULATE TONGUES

I have personally witnessed that when I pray in tongues, there are moments I speak foreign languages that I know are spoken by other groups of people. If those people might be around they would interpret what I speak. I have no idea how I manage to say words in those languages. It's only God who enables me.

I listened to a believer who was speaking in tongues

but her utterance kept on changing from one articulate language to another and switching back and forth. I encouraged her to record those "other" tongues and show them to people speaking those languages to help interpret them. And they did.

These kinds of tongues we can refer to as *articulate*— expressive, coherent and well-spoken languages but foreign to the one uttering. The person speaking in articulate tongues does not understand them unless God interprets them for him. However, any person speaking one of those languages will be able to translate without a special gift from God.

For example, during the day of Pentecost, the disciples were able to speak foreign languages (xenolalia) that they were not speaking before but spoken by different nationalities. Luckily some of the people from those nationalities were around and confirmed it. They knew these people in the upper room were Galileans and not native speakers of those languages. "Now when this was announced, the multitude came together, and were confounded, because every man heard them speak in his own language." (Acts 2:6)

If you are already baptized in the Spirit and speak in tongues, work on sharpening your tongues speaking until you are able to utter articulate languages. These languages don't necessarily need a special interpreter, for anyone who understands them can interpret them. But if no one who knows that language is available, then seek God for interpretation.

Those articulate tongues are not permanent languages to the one speaking. They may come once according to the intensions of the Spirit within. Pastor Emmanuel Twagirimana, who died during the Rwandan Genocide and came back to life after seven days was able to speak Swedish for few days despite the fact that he knew only the language(s) of his native country, Rwanda.

We have already noted the two classifications of tongues: *prophetic,* meant to edify the church and *communal,* meant to commune with God. So "speaking in tongues" emphasizes prophetic utterance to edify the church when interpreted. (I Cor. 14:5) "Praying in tongues" stresses communal communication with God from within the human spirit (v.14), and may not necessarily need interpretation since it is a prayer that is offered to God using supernatural language understood by God alone.

On the other hand, if you are filled in the Holy Spirit, try to balance your tongues speaking. Don't restrict your tongues to asyllabic form; rather alter your speaking both in tongues and in understanding. If Paul could alter his prayers and singing, we can do it too as the Spirit leads.

Furthermore, don't only pray in tongues for less than five minutes and conclude your prayers. You may not reach to the "threshold" to receive revelations. Many "fiery" ministers of God testify of receiving word of knowledge, prophecies and interpretation of tongues usually after spending quality time praying.

Remember Jesus would spend hours alone praying, sometimes the whole night. He knew the secret of spending enough time with God. Before embarking on His ministry, He spent forty days and nights in the wilderness in a fast. (Matt. 4:2)

The night before His arrest, He also spent quality time praying until His sweat turned to blood. (Luke 22:41-47) Why did His "sweat" turn to blood? It means Jesus' prayers reached a miracle threshold embodying

His special mission to save the world.

In the African jungles, when hunters want fire and they don't have matchboxes or the like, they usually devise other plans. They get two dry sticks, put one stick on smashed dry grass, and use the other stick for rubbing to cause friction. They will rub it harder until smoke comes out and then fire begins. Rubbing demands effort and must continue until fire is realized.

Take time in prayers especially in tongues until your "rubbing" becomes so hot that supernatural fire is evidenced and there you will be able to hear Him vividly. Continue praying "with" the spirit until you are able to pray "in" the *Spirit*. Do you understand what I mean? Read the first part of 1 Corinthians 14:15 and Ephesians 6:18 to understand the connotation of praying both with the spirit and in the Holy Spirit.

Pastor David Yonggi Cho, the founder of *Yoido Full Gospel Church* in South Korea tells of the time he desperately needed God's answer for the future of his church. He prayed with his executive for about two hours but nothing happened. After dismissing the rest of the pastors, he again continued to pray for more than two hours, specifically in tongues. It was at that moment when God began to speak to him clearly telling him the future of his church. Today he has the biggest congregation in the world with over one million members in attendance.

Unpleasantly, I know of a certain Spirit-filled believer who speaks the same syllable every time he utters a tongue. He would make that monosyllabic sound for ten seconds and then begin it afresh; he would repeat it again until prayers are concluded. Anything we are not serious in learning we will definitely remain stagnant, no progress at all.

God can give you a new utterance if you are willing and eager to receive the gift. It's not for you to invent such utterances as some always do, but allow God to use your faculties to bring blessings.

DYNAMICS OF SPEAKING WORDLESS GROANINGS

Romans 8 especially verse 26 has puzzled many Bible reading believers. The way Apostle Paul reveals prayer here looks unusual to the types of tongues speaking I mentioned earlier in this section. For example, in Acts 2:4 we are told the Spirit of God came on the disciples and gave them divine *utterance* where they spoke the prompted utterance in "articulate" languages. Also in 1 Corinthians 14 particularly in verses 2, 4, 9, 14 and 27 Paul reveals another trend of tongues speaking that is uttered out in a "gibberish" mode—not in articulate language thus calling for interpretation when done in church.

But the kind of praying revealed in Romans 8:26 looks unique and classic to all other kinds of *uttered* tongues. The one revealed here *"cannot be uttered."* It is the Holy Spirit making the prayers Himself in us and in His own way and timing.

Paul says, "Likewise the Spirit also *helps in our weaknesses.* For we do not know what we should pray for as we ought, *but the Spirit Himself makes intercession for us* with *groanings* which *cannot be uttered"* (NKJV emphasis italicized).

To understand this sweet passage well, several points need to be examined. First, the verse reveals that the Spirit of God *helps in our weakness.* The English word "helps" is here translated from the Greek word **sunantilambanomai**—meaning "to take hold with at the side or to supply help that exactly corresponds to the need." So the Spirit of God helps us by interceding in accordance to our personal needs individually.

Paul painted the infamous feebleness of human mind

in connection to ultimate understanding, recounting and knowing as "weakness" or "infirmity." The Spirit knows any prayer that comes from the mind is weak thus lacks ultimate expression.

Second, *the Spirit Himself makes intercession for us.* Meaning the Spirit stands on our behalf and speaks on our behalf as an advocate or a lawyer presenting a client's case before court (John 14:16). Unlike praying or speaking in tongues where we cooperate with Him by praying using our "spirit" but here the Holy Spirit takes charge and prays by Himself in us.

Third, the Spirit intercedes for us *with groanings which cannot be uttered.* The word "groanings" is here translated from the Greek word *stenagmois*—meaning a "sigh or cry brought by a great pressure." There is actually a force forcing this inexpressive sound out *(alalétos)*. That kind of groaning cannot be spoken out in form of words; it's too deep to express in words.

As we noted earlier, speaking in tongues comes in diverse forms—gibbering or articulating—the kind of intercession Paul is talking abut in Romans cannot be uttered. It is the Spirit of God taking sole domination over our sensory faculties in conformity to the divine law of spirit entrance into the natural.

Those who are filled with the Holy Spirit and pray in

tongues *regularly* can testify that, there are moments when they woke up from sleep they would find themselves groaning in prayer, fully "electrified" in the power of the Holy Ghost as they mutter.

Over two years ago I suddenly woke up from sleep and found myself laboring in prayer through groaning. After everything was done, I went back to sleep. To my surprise, I was woken up by my landlord and police. It was around 7 o'clock in the morning. The police examined me to see if I was safe. I didn't understand why they did that and what was happening.

When I came out from my bedroom, I found four doors leading into my room were all broken badly by armed robbers. The robbers reached into my room while I was asleep but they never touched me nor stole any valuables.

Who protected me and how did it happen? The Spirit of God already interceded for me using prophetic groaning. If I was to use my own mind and method of prayer, I would have known nothing and I am not sure if I would have survived.

On a similar manner, a woman was once going to prayer meeting and on the way she began to cry, mumble, mutter and groan uncontrollably and attracted a number of onlookers. Later, when she came back home, she found thieves had broken into her house but they never took anything. They were repulsed by angels and ran in a disarray. The Spirit of God knew exactly what was happening and interceded for the lady.

Allowing the Holy Spirit to take full charge in us brings ultimate protection and great success indeed. Diversifying your prayers from tongues into the threshold of wordless groanings is paramount. Pastor Christ Oyakhilome of *Christ Embassy* calls it the "highest level of prayer" and calls our attention to embrace it.

In Acts 19:11-12 we see amazing miracles wrought by an ordinary man: "And God wrought special miracles by the hands of Paul: So that from his body were brought unto the sick handkerchiefs or aprons, and the diseases departed from them, and the evil spirits went out of them."

It was not because he was an apostle. Paul actually soaked himself in a "certain" kind of continuous praying where his spirit, soul and body were *subdued* by the Holy Ghost and anything coming in contact with him became extraordinary. In other words, the Spirit of God that lives within the spirit of Paul came out in full to do the work Himself.

Such amazing miracles still happen today. Have you ever seen ministers of God getting "drunk" in the Holy Spirit, whereby when they raise their hands or declare words, people begin falling, shivering and evil spirits manifesting? Kenneth Hagin was ministering in a church and called volunteers to take the microphone from his hand to conclude the service, but no one was able to grab it or even come close to him—they were falling and shaking vigorously.

Pastor Chris demonstrated what Apostle Peter did by his shadow. Chris passed near the congregation and the moment his shadow touched them, they began to fall on the ground. Benny Hinn would fling his coat and a multitude would fall, shaking vigorously.

Last year, we held a conference in the USA and one of the ministers, Pastor Anthony Lupai, gave his Bible for the choir to hold but no one was able to hold it—everyone that touched the Bible fell on the ground, shaking and babbling.

Such demonstrations have puzzled many people today—they wonder how and where is that power coming from; is it from satan or from God?

When the Spirit of the Lord manifests in full in your life, anything you say, touch or do is a miracle itself. You can anoint handkerchiefs, water, oil or objects and they will deliver and heal people.

But this happens only when we master how to stay in the secret place of the Most High, allowing the Holy Spirit to subdue every faculty of ours for His glory. "Insomuch that they brought forth the sick into the streets, and laid them on beds and couches, that at the least the shadow of Peter passing by might overshadow some of them." (Acts 5:15)

CHAPTER 5

RECOGNIZE SENSORY CHANNELS

The Bible assures believers in Christ that the Spirit of God has taken their body as His abode to manifest His glory. (1 Cor. 3:16) This simply means God lives inside us and can speak in us using our sensory faculties. He wants to share everything within us.

We don't have to wait, look up in the sky to see God with our natural eyes coming in the clouds to speak to us with a roaring thunderous voice as it happened at Mount Sinai. (Ex. 19:16-19) God can drop His words inside us and expects our sensory faculties to bring them out as we pray. They could come in various forms—through thoughts, sensations, impressions or rhema word.

For instance, when we take food into our body, we expect the nutritious contents to be absorbed to nourish us while expecting the residues to come out through excretion. Similarly, as God dwells in us, He first nourishes our inner beings with the divine food (Matt. 4:4) and the bonuses are then emitted out in the form of rhema word as per our focus here. That spoken word does edify the church and convict sinners to embrace Christ.

When the Canaanite woman exchanged words with Jesus, He told her, "It is not right to take the children's bread and give it to the dogs." (Matt. 15:26 ERV) Interestingly she replied, "Yes, Lord, but even the dogs eat the pieces of food that fall from their master's table." Jesus conceded as she insisted and He provided her request with rapturous commendation. (v.28)

Jesus knew He was specifically sent first to the chosen people of Israel who were privileged to take the Light into the world. They were redeemed and brought out from Egypt into the Promised Land flowing with milk and honey. They should first enjoy the divine food prepared for them and then extend that to other nations. Jesus knew after His Ascension the door would be officially opened to the Gentiles to enjoy in the same way as the biological children of Abraham.

It's true, after Ascension Paul was chosen to be an

apostle to the Gentiles preparing the table ready for all to eat—not crumbs any more. "For God, who was at work in Peter as an apostle to the circumcised, *was also at work in me as an apostle to the Gentiles.*" (Gal. 2:8 NIV emphasis italicized)

The spiritual food of God is now inside you. Prepare a table through your prayers to commune with the Giver. The "crumbs" falling from inside you should be released— through prophecies, deliverance, healing and miracles. Just open those sensory organs ready to receive the rhema word from within and release it.

When prophets in the Bible declare prophecies, how did they receive them? Were they feeling some divine urges or the words were actually whispered into them by God?

As we continue reading this chapter, we will find out several modes God uses to communicate His messages to His people especially when praying in tongues. Let's ask God to open our understanding so that we will be able to hear Him and develop a constant connection with Him every day.

HEARING GOD THROUGH SENSORY ORGANS

God takes our five senses and uses them to convey His message to us especially when we are speaking in tongues. Speaking in tongues is a quick and easy way to hear God. It is better than waiting to go to sleep so that God can come in a dream or vision to speak to us when our mind is put to rest leaving room for our spirit to commune.

When you steadfastly pray in tongues, you will be able to hear God right away. It's just like going to a drive-thru restaurant where everything is readily prepared just awaiting your order. You don't have to go to the counter, order your food and sit down to wait while it's being prepared. No, it's a quick transaction.

Tongues invoke God to speak to you on the spot because you are just collecting His messages that have been already dropped into your inner man.

Science has informed us that the five human senses are equipped with certain types of sensory cells capable of communicating messages in peculiar demeanors. Our eyes are equipped with *ophthalmoception* senses to see things, the ears are equipped with the senses of *audioception* to hear sounds, our tongues have *gustaoception* senses to taste things, our nose also have *olfacception* senses to smell odors and the skin is equipped with *actioception* for feeling. God also uses them to communicate to us.

When you are praying don't be negligent of any inclinations you may be encountering. Learn ways to switch off your mind to give freedom to your spirit to bring out those "nuggets" dropped inside your spirit by the Spirit of God. We call those inclinations "prompts" because they are stimulated by divine power within to manifest in our senses.

Ophthalmoception: Seeing Things When Speaking in Tongues

Jesus once told the Pharisee opposing Him that He only does what He "sees" the Father doing. (John 5:19) Check out when He multiplied the two fish and five loaves that fed over five thousand people, plus women and children. He began to thank God for the miracle when it was still two fish and five pieces of bread. (Luke 9:16) Jesus *had already* seen the Father multiplying the fish and bread even before He lifted them up. He already saw the miracle before it happened physically.

Why was the Prophet Elisha peaceful when his

attackers surrounded him? He *already saw in the spirit* the protecting force from heaven defending him. Elisha's servant was afraid because he didn't see anything but the enemies. His peace came only after his eyes were opened through Elisha's prayers to see the supporting force. (2 Kings 6:15-17)

If we train ourselves to sense the movement of the Spirit in our lives as we attune ourselves to speaking in tongues, we will receive great results. God will open our eyes and we will be able to see things in the spirit.

If you are praying in tongues and suddenly see flushes of images, people, scenes or objects in the spirit be alert— God might be telling you something.

Pastor Jerame Nelson was ministering and in the spirit he suddenly saw five deaf people coming forward to receive healing. However, when he opened his eyes and looked around no one was standing at the front. Immediately, he remembered what Jesus said that He does what He sees the Father doing in heaven. He then boldly called five blind men to come forward for healing. Shockingly, they responded and God healed them all. This was followed by several healings of different diseases.

Pastor Jonathan Welton was in the Seattle area to

pray for a woman suffering from cancer whose doctors believed she would die within weeks. When Pastor Welton began to pray for her, God opened his spiritual eyes and saw demonic spears, arrows and horrible weapons piercing through the woman thus causing great pains.

When he began to pray for the woman he saw angels removing those cancerous weapons one after the other. After the removal he then declared healing of the wounds.

The woman slept peacefully that night and woke up perfectly healed. The cancer was no more.

As we keep praying in tongues and attune ourselves to sense the movement of the Spirit within us we will definitely "see" in the spirit. But it will only happen when we take time to train ourselves to easily switch into the spirit realm without interruptions.

The power of God lives in you and if you become the temple of God then commune with the Spirit. You don't have to pray, preach, sing or serve God blindly without seeing. Make all efforts to decode the special messages of God in your tongues speaking.

Audioception: Hearing Things When Speaking in Tongues

King Saul was commanded by God not to spare any Amalekite including their animals. (1 Sam. 15:3) But instead he spared the king and the best animals and yet lied to the Prophet Samuel telling Samuel he had fulfilled the mission God commanded him. (v.13) But the Prophet Samuel perceived the opposite: "And Samuel said, What meaneth then this *bleating* of the sheep in mine ears, and the *lowing* of the oxen which I hear?" (v.14 emphasis italicized)

The "bleating" and "lowing" sound revealed the secret King Saul concealed from Samuel. (v.24) Prophet Samuel *heard* the sound of the animals in his inner man and knew the King disobeyed God even though he denied it. When King Saul realized the secret was revealed, he had to confess but tried to justify his actions.

Hearing the voice of God in prayer is common to believers who acknowledge the mysterious operations of the Spirit. The prophets in the Bible received their calling by hearing the voice of God directly, rather than someone telling them or prophesying to them like is the practice today.

God appeared to Saul, who later became Paul, on the way to Damascus (Acts 9:1-8) when the light shone on him and all fell to the ground. Jesus challenged Saul's murderous missions and gave him an alternative. But "those who were with me saw the light, but did not understand the voice of the One who was speaking to me." (Acts 22:9 AMP) Saul was the only one who heard Jesus speaking to him in Hebrew (Acts 26:14 NKJV) while those with him heard only a voice rather than words even though they knew Hebrew and Aramaic.

On another point Jesus says, "My sheep hear my voice, and I know them, and they follow me." (John 10:27) If we don't clearly hear the voice of God, then our being as followers of Jesus Christ is questionable—something somewhere is missing. I know of many believers, who, when they encounter some phenomenon they get confused; they don't know if it is God or satan talking to them. In all your walk with the Lord try to acquaint yourself with His voice so that you will be able to clearly hear Him.

Gustaoception: Tasting Things When Speaking in Tongues

There are several Bible verses and contemporary testimonies of believers reporting the eating and tasting of valuables in the realm of the spirit. Physically, those valuables may not be eaten. When satan tempted Jesus to misuse His power to turn stones into bread Jesus correlated the bread into spiritual food useful for living. (Matt. 4:4)

There are some moments God feeds His ministers with the Bible as their food to taste its sweetness. Ezekiel was given a scroll to eat; he did eat and the taste in his mouth was "as honey for sweetness." (Ezek. 3:3) After enjoying the sweetness, God paradoxically said it was His word that He put in his mouth to speak out.

When you are praying in the spirit, not just only in dreams and vision, you may be able to taste things in the spirit. But all these things have meanings. A couple of years ago, after prayers I was given a Bible in a vision to eat and I did eat. I later understood the connotation behind that experience. I knew God "packed' His words inside me to spread out to nations through preaching, teaching, writing or exercising. This book you are reading is a result of that experience.

God has called us all to taste how good He is and we should always trust His words spoken to us. He says, "O taste and see that the LORD is good: blessed is the man that trusteth in him." (Ps. 34:8) This proceeds from the mouth of Jesus: "Very truly I tell you, unless you eat the flesh of the Son of Man and drink his blood, you have no life in you." (John 6:53 NIV)

I have been asked several times by "occasional" Christians to reveal the secret why many of us enjoy prayers and fellowship. Some of them told me they couldn't spend long time praying, for they would feel bored and run out of expressive words. Even regular church attendance was unbearable for them.

I simply encouraged them to desire the ultimate praying "appetizer" to get filled in the power of the Holy Spirit to enable them speak in tongues then they would enjoy encountering God.

Sadly, many professing Christians report of eating disgusting food in dreams which is being forced into them by certain forces. When they wake up from sleep some of them become sick, silly and lose opportunities. They are being initiated by satan. For satan likes to pervert holy ways of God in order to make us doubt our Creator. If you encounter satan in such a manner, rebuke him right away. He will leave you.

Nevertheless, any pervasive thing that comes from satan can be known right away unless otherwise some of us are not actually sheep. For Jesus says, "My sheep

hear my voice, and I know them, and they follow me."
(John 10:27)

Olfacception: Smelling Things When Speaking in Tongues

When you enter a deserted room even though your eyes are blindfolded you can, by smelling, know that no one is staying in that room. You don't need an explanation for the olfacception gland has already told you.

This too can happen in the realm of the spirit when we train ourselves to attune our smelling glands to sense substances in the spirit.

In the Old Testament when sacrifices were to be offered to God, priests would add frankincense and myrrh to cause a sweet aroma before the Lord. (Ex. 30:7-9) Similarly, the wise men from the East brought quality incense to the child Jesus as they worshipped Him. (Matt. 2:11)

Eschatologically, the Apostle John sees angels burning incense in a censer before the throne of God mixing with prayers of the saints. (Rev. 8:3-4)

Even today the Roman Catholic and Orthodox priests, among others, do practice incense burning when ministering.

All these show the "figurative" importance of sweet smell the Lord loves.

Therefore, smelling things in the spirit is common today. If you pray in tongues and begin to smell things in the spirit be alert to those inclinations. God might be sending you a message to decode.

Pastor Alph from Johannesburg, South Africa, was speaking in tongues and called a believer to the altar for specific prayers. But as she was approaching, an unusual odor emanated from her for just few seconds. The pastor asked her about the meaning of that smell. She was shocked and began to thank God for identifying the devil attacking her family.

She narrated that when she was on the verge of succeeding, her house roof, particularly her room would start smelling so nasty, forcing them to vacate it for a while. The following days everything she would touch was just a disappointment and failure. The odor would disappear for a while awaiting breakthrough moments.

When the Pastor touched her, demons began to manifest and confessed they caused the smell. Fortunately, they were expelled by the authority of Jesus.

How did Pastor Alph identify the actual cause of the disappointment of that believer in which demons began to manifest? It was through spiritual *smelling*. The congregation and in particular, those near the Pastor smelled nothing. The smell was sensed in the spirit by a particular person. It was not a physical odor.

If you sharpen your inner man properly the Spirit of God can do amazing things in your life. You become "another prophet" for the glory of God. The veil that hinder us from entering into the Holy of Holies is torn (Heb. 10:19-22), we can go now direct to "scoop" rhema words that come in various forms including smelling. The Apostle Peter quoting Joel 2:28 said, "And it shall come to pass in the last days, saith God, I will pour out of my Spirit upon all flesh: and your sons and your daughters shall prophesy, and your young men shall see visions, and your old men shall dream dreams." (Acts 2:17)

Tactioception: Feeling Things When Speaking in Tongues

When you are praying in tongues, have you ever felt some sensation in your body? Pastor Jerame Nelson testified that many times when he would go to his usual grocery shop with his wife, he would feel an unusual surge in his right hand. But he had no idea what to do about it. His wife believed God wanted him to pray for someone at the grocery. They looked around and saw a crippled woman in a wheel chair. Jerame approached her and asked if she would agree him pray for her. She agreed.

When he laid his "electrified" right hand on the lady, she felt an electric shock and instantly stood up and began to walk without any support. All of them were shocked.

A new believer asked me how some ministers would know there is a specific pain in people and then call them out for prayers? I told her God works in different ways. But one way is that you may feel some weird pains in one area of your body which is actually a message God is telling you someone is experiencing such pain. If you are keen and bold enough to call anyone with such pain out, a person will show up with the exact pain.

A week later, during Friday prayer meeting, that same believer experienced a weird pain and asked the pastor to call anyone with an excruciating pain in the left shoulder. One person came forward for prayer and they were both surprised that God talked to them. The person who came forward was prayed for and the pain left.

These testimonies can help us learn some of the mysterious ways God speaks to us during a service. Your divine surge maybe different from this one but recognize how God works in you.

The woman with a blood issue wanted to only touch the apparel of Jesus to receive her healing. She did it among the crowd and received her healing. Jesus felt "Somebody hath touched me: for I perceive that virtue is gone out of me." (Luke 8:46) Peter was disturbed with the question because many people pressed on Jesus. But later the woman identified herself and fell on Jesus feet narrating the entire story and how she got healed. (v.47) In fact, Jesus felt that touch in His spirit and knew "virtue" had gone out of Him to heal some body having great faith.

Have you ever felt the presence of God in your body directing you to pray or do some divine intervention? Always recognize the movement of God in your life. The more you recognize Him the more frequently you will hear Him and walk in His ways.

HEARING GOD THROUGH YOUR SPIRIT

Sometimes when you wake up from sleep and your spirit urges you to pray don't hesitate, just pray. You may not know why you are prompted to do so. It might be preventing something evil happening to others or yourself.

Even in your sleep when you receive some messages from dreams or visions don't ignore them, but acknowledge them. It could be God trying to tell you something. The moment you continue recognizing certain prompts God will be inclined to talk to you regularly and interpretation of tongues will be stress-free.

Dreams or visions that God gives are different from ordinary dreams that come from satan or within us due to some indulgences.

Several days ago I needed a help concerning an important matter, I called several people but they were busy. So I resorted to praying as well as singing in the spirit. Suddenly a random thought came into my mind out of blue, saying I should call so and so. I realized it was God answering me.

I asked the Lord in English to tell me what to say to the person. In my spirit, the Lord told me to ask about that person's calendar. I called him and did exactly as God prompted. We arranged important matters that helped me a lot. How wonderful it is to adhere to God's voice.

I would have suffered and called a wrong person if I used my ordinary thinking.

During my counseling class, my professor encouraged us to be always alert on certain statements, postures, words, expressions or face messages that clients tend to portray during counseling session. They may lead to the core of the issue and show where clients need the help. But if you ignore and only go with the literal way of statements, you may end nowhere.

Similar, be keen to recognize unusual things coming your way when praying in tongues or ministering. They can lead you to great moments.

Random Thoughts When Speaking in Tongues

Have you ever thought of a friend you have not met for a period and as you start thinking about that friend, to your surprise, the friend shows up unexpectedly or calls you? Humanly speaking, such an event seems peculiar. Why is your friend showing at the time you were thinking or talking about him?

Science, however, admits such trends but fails to ascertain the cause of the coincidence. Psychology calls that meaningful coincident *synchronicity*—an acausal connecting principle.

This means the "meaningful coincident" is actually taking place in the spirit realm.

The Lord says, "Commit thy works unto the LORD, and thy thoughts shall be established." (Prov. 16:3) So praying in tongues helps our mind to position itself towards the very essence of God's heart. Our thoughts shall be established to retrieve the divine plan of God necessary for our daily life.

Dr. Oral Roberts established the world-renowned charismatic university, Oral Roberts University, through praying in tongues. God spoke to him as he was praying and listening to the voice of God. By faith he took the thought seriously thus resulting in the successful establishment of the University.

Many friends of mine who speak in tongues do tell me that when they pray with the spirit their mind sometimes distracts them. Their mind wanders all over, thinking, imagining and seeing junk stuff contrary to the praying mood. They wonder if this could hinder the inflow of the Holy Spirit in them.

It's true, this is one of the main reasons Spirit filled believers don't hear God even though they speak in tongues. If you always experience this devilish distraction, train your mind to conform to the Word of God rather than become a liability to hearing God. (Rom.12:2)

Pastor Alph Lukau of *Alleluia Ministries International* in South Africa, who often prophesies to people by calling their names, birth days, addresses and telling them exactly their personal issues encourages those praying in tongues to train their mind to imagine God, angels or the love of God when praying with the spirit to avoid negative thinking.

He also encourages those who are quite mature in the things of the Spirit to do a parallel praying as well. He means when you continue praying in tongues, if at the same time you see in your mind somebody you know or your church, then do intercessory prayer using your mind.

Some may think it is very hard to do parallel praying. But I would say if musicians can use their hands on key keyboard or guitar while leading in singing at the same time, you can also do parallel praying. It's just a matter of practice.

It's also important to meditate on scriptures before praying in order to position your mind on the right track. When you are praying in tongues and your mind wanders away, come back to your meditated verse and speak it out loudly as you continue praying. You will find yourself disciplining your mind to conform to the praying mood.

Random Words When Speaking in Tongues

When you speak in tongues or even sing with the spirit you will expose yourself to experiences you never imagined. Words may come into your subjective senses. Don't ignore them.

Rev. Michael Yemba, the founder of *Jesus Is Lord Ministries for All Nations*, invited guests to speak in a conference in Dallas, Texas. During his morning devotions he found himself repeating certain word every time he was praying in tongues.

At the eve of the conference he went to the airport to pick up one of the guest speakers. The bishop had come from South Africa together with his spiritual son, called

Shadung. The wife of the Reverend recalled and reminded him, "Pastor do you remember every morning during your devotions you kept on mentioning the name 'Shadung' and we wondered what it was about?" They then realized that Reverend Yemba was interceding for Apostle Shadung's visa case among other issues.

Speaking in tongues is prophetic and can save many lives and situations.

When you are praying in tongues and you keep repeating certain words, take note of them.

Do you know that the definition of rhema is Spirit's *spoken* word for the *now?* It is an utterance of God's voice. (Acts 11:16) *Speaking in tongues is a quick access to the rhema word.* Jesus tells His disciples in John 6: 63 that, "the words that I speak unto you, they are spirit, and they are life."

If God speaks to you then those words can make your life successful. Those words maybe calling you for repentance, forgiveness or new appointments.

Not only that, the moment you become expectant to wanting God speak to you, He will do it.

We don't have to expect a roaring voice of God like at Mount Sinai. (Ex. 19:14-19) God may be talking to us daily in a still voice and if we are not sure we are ignoring His voice. "And after the earthquake a fire; but the LORD was not in the fire: and after the fire a still small voice. And it was so, when Elijah heard it, that he wrapped his face in his mantle, and went out, and stood in the entrance of the cave. And, behold, there came a voice unto him, and said, What doest thou here, Elijah?" (1 Kings 19:12-13)

Random Statements When Speaking in Tongues

Through the praying process, be keen to consider random statements that come from your inner man. When you are under the influence of the Holy Ghost you will definitely utter some statements that have not been prepared by your mind. They come from a different source—your spirit.

One time Kenneth Hagin spoke in tongues during Sunday service and declared many projects he was going to undertake. When they came home, his wife asked him when the Bible school he spoke about would be built. He was surprised and denied to have said anything as such.

His wife insisted and asked him to prove by listening to the recorded tape of the sermon. He listened and heard himself declaring he was going to open a Bible school to be named Rhema Bible College.

Just because of that revelation through tongues, today Rhema Bible College has graduated thousands of students and many of them have become clergymen.

When Paul was on his way to Rome by ship he perceived danger in his spirit about the voyage. Paul said unto them, "Sirs, *I perceive that this voyage* will be with hurt and much damage, not only of the lading and ship, but also of our lives." (Acts 27:10 emphasis italicized) Later his words were proven right. (v.21)

Paul was not seeing this upcoming danger through his mind but rather through his spirit. He didn't care if people would agree with him or not. It's true no one took his advice. They trusted the experience of the pilot and the owner of the ship (v.11) but the outcome proved them wrong and favored Paul's spiritual perception.

I was once ministering and during prayer time a random thought came to me. I spoke it out without disputing the source. But few minutes later my mind began to rationalize what I spoke and started rebuking me to have said it without analyzing.

When I came down from the podium, a believer approached me saying the statement I made was exactly what he was undergoing. If he had told someone, he would have thought I heard it from that person.

Again another member told me the statement I made

answered her issue precisely.

If I hesitated from speaking those random statements right away, my mind would prevent me and those members wouldn't be helped.

But we have to be wise in saying things unnecessarily. All procedures of tongues and spiritual ventures—words of knowledge, faith, prophecy, interpretation—go along with wisdom. Pray for the gift of wisdom to be given you. *Wisdom is the essence of decency and can protect your life in difficult choices.* It helps in deciding when and how to speak or approach things.

CHAPTER 6

SEEK DECODING PRUDENCE

Jesus tells us in John 15:7 that, "If you abide in Me, and My words abide in you, you will ask what you desire, and it shall be done for you." Jesus here gives two "abiding" conditions for our desires to be given us.

First is to abide or remain in Him—meaning staying connected with Him at all times through prayers and communing.

Second is to embrace the Word of God so it becomes our sole language, stirring the mind to conform into the perfect intentions God has for us. As we fulfill these conditions then we will be able to ask the Father for our desires and we will receive them.

If we desire the gift of tongues interpretation while dwelling in the secret place, we will receive the gift. Some Christians tell me that the gift of interpretation of tongues is only given to whomever God wishes, not for them. The reason is they sought for the gift but to no avail and they have now stopped seeking.

The gift of interpretation of tongues is as the gift of faith. For instance, God said that He has "not given us a spirit of fear, but of power and of love and of a sound mind." (2 Tim. 1:7) Meaning **deilias** (fear) is a spirit sent from a different source other than God. On the other hand, **dunameos** (power), **agapes** (love) and **sophronismou** (sound mind) are distinct spirit(s) sent from God.

Isaiah 11:2 also gives us certain gifts of the Spirit that would prophetically be given to "someone" coming from the stem of Jesse. "And the spirit of the LORD shall rest upon him, the spirit of wisdom and understanding, the spirit of counsel and might, the spirit of knowledge and of the fear of the LORD."

When King Solomon asked God to bless him with wisdom and knowledge (2 Chron. 1:10) God, in addition, added other precious gifts to enable him to execute his duties efficiently. Then God said, "Wisdom and knowledge is granted unto thee; and *I will give thee riches, and wealth, and honour,* such as none of the kings have had that have been before thee, neither shall there any after thee have the like." (v.12 additional gifts italicized for emphasis)

All the mentioned gifts above are distinct in operation, but sometimes come in pairs. If the spirit of wisdom and understanding come in pairs, then speaking in tongues can come along with the spirit of interpretation to some extent. Even in 1 Corinthians 12:10 they are linked to each other and put all in one verse.

Often the frustration we have today comes of failing to receive what we want from God because we "shout from a far" when God is not "near." We don't seek Him *first* before calling Him to grant us our desires. "Seek ye the LORD while he may be found, call ye upon him while he is near." (Isa. 55:6)

RECOGNIZE UNIQUE SENSATIONS

God might have already endowed you with interpretation skills but you may be unaware. Jeremiah was ordained a prophet by God but he didn't know it. Instead he urged God to send someone else because he was young and couldn't speak well. (Jer. 1:6)

Moses tried to refuse God's calling to leadership because of his ineloquence. (Ex. 4:11) He didn't know the stick in his hand was anointed for supernatural acts—he thought it was "just" a walking stick. "And the LORD said unto him, What is that in thine hand? And he said, A rod. And he said, Cast it on the ground. And he cast it on the ground, and it became a serpent; and Moses fled from before it." (v.2-3)

There is some anointing in you that you have no idea about. Believe and act on whatever opportunity God gives you and you will see His hands on you doing amazing things. You are not just a "walking stick," but an anointed fellow to do the supernatural with the gift God has already placed in you. Recognize it.

Gideon was a mighty warrior who delivered Israel from the hands of Midianites but didn't know he had that power. Instead, he looked back into his family background and used it as an excuse until God corrected him. (Judges 6:12-16)

Are you exceptional? If you can speak in tongues, then you can interpret your tongues too when it's meant for prophecy. "Wherefore let him that speaketh in an unknown tongue pray that he may interpret." (1 Cor. 14:13) God cannot give a gift without remedying it with another gift if the demand requires. If you keep missing God's voice, the blame is yours not God's, not even the devil's.

Kenneth Hagin once told how he had a vision where he had the chance of meeting Jesus talking to him. However, the devil stood next to Hagin making a lot of noisy interruptions. But Jesus kept on talking until Hagin asked Jesus to send the devil away so that he could hear Him clearly.

Instead Jesus told Hagin the authority and power to cast demons out has already been given to believers; it was up to Hagin. Jesus kept talking again and the devil continued distracting. When Hagin realized the power he had been given, he commanded the devil out and the devil vanished immediately. Then he was able to hear Jesus clearly.

If you pray in tongues don't allow distractions from the mind to distort your praying. Seek the Lord and get knowledge. The Lord says, "You will seek me and find me when you seek me with all your heart." (Jer. 29:13 NIV)

The English word *seek* where Jeremiah uses here is the Hebrew word **baqash** which refers to eager desiring, inquiring, investigating, looking for, pursuing, searching something until it is obtained.

Seeking persuades us to explore God deeper without

giving up. Study your Bible especially in areas pertaining to your desires. If you want God to give you the gift of interpretation, prepare the ground ready to usher in this special gift. You cannot throw seeds into a bushy place and expect a harvest later. Clean the place and make it well prepared.

Make use of the Bible to educate yourself about tongues so that interpretation will be ushered into a prepared place. God cannot give us something that doesn't suit our stature. He wants to train us first to clear a space for the gift to settle in.

Moses is a typical example. God took him to Pharaoh's palace to learn protocols and get the best education. (Acts 7:22) He had to be in the wilderness for forty years to learn leadership and trust in the Lord in areas which wouldn't have been addressed at Pharaoh's house. When he was ready then God called him to lead even though he couldn't believe in himself yet. (Ex. 3)

As you continue seeking God to anoint you with the gift of interpretation, believe that you have received and "stay' in the believing stage. Don't be like many Christians who pray for something and after thanking God claiming to have received and then they revert to the "seeking" stage again. It becomes a cycle.

A pastor was diagnosed with deadly sickness and his doctors told him he would only live for few weeks. That pastor claimed miracles have ceased. But now death was threatening him and forcing him to explore the Bible without using people's ideas put into doctrines.

He decided to take a vacation from the church for two weeks. He was living alone in his farmland just studying the Word on areas of healing. The scriptures convinced him that healing still exists. He wrote those verses down and began to declare them into his life. Shortly he met notable guests in a certain gathering and told them he was healed, but the pain was still there.

The guests asked him to go with them for a hike because he was healed already. He reluctantly accepted and the moment he started climbing the mountain, the pain became excruciating and his breath was getting shorter. The memorized scriptures kept popping in his mind and he began to declare those healing verses every moment while thanking God about his healing. But the pain and exhaustion continued till they came down from the hill.

Suddenly within the twinkling of an eye, the pain disappeared and he was healed completely. His testimony changed the lives of many people.

How did he get healed? By reading scriptures, and declaring them as remedy to his sickness. He stood on his confession without wavering. Satan tried to whisper to him so that he would doubt God but the scriptures he kept declaring revived him till healing happened.

As you seek God for interpretation He will definitely give you some hints of the results through convictions, dreams and visions.

Many online streams today are helpful to educate us on subjects we want to explore. Don't miss them, find good preachers online and read good books. Listen to them and compare everything they do with the Bible to help you be on track. You have to know that all people talking about God are not His disciples, they maybe wolves coming in sheep's skin.

TRANSCRIBE PROMPTED UTTERANCES

Bible writers were inspired by the Holy Spirit to write scriptures and hence they diligently acted promptly. Today we see the result of their work in the form of the Bible. They knew God was speaking through them to inspire others in their writings which are passed to us.

God told the Apostle John to write down what he saw and send it to the seven churches in Asia Minor. He did it. Thus he says, 'I was in the Spirit on the Lord's Day, and I heard behind me a loud voice, as of a trumpet, saying, "I am the Alpha and the Omega, the First and the Last," and, "What you see, write in a book and send *it* to the seven churches which are in Asia."' (Rev. 1:10-11)

I recently received a "moving" testimony from someone in Houston, Texas, who read my book entitled *Power*. He took three days off from work just to have enough time to read my book. The following Sunday he came to his church testifying what God did in his life through the book. If I hadn't transcribed my understanding and experiences, he would not have experienced that trend.

A certain Christian at our watch was filled with the Holy Spirit and began to speak articulate tongues, she was so curious about what she was saying in tongues. She decided to record her tongues and asked us to listen and identify those languages she was uttering. We identified Amharic (Ethiopian), Hebrew, Chinese and Arabic among others.

She then consulted people who speak those languages and made them listen to the recorded voice. Amazingly all of them, though consulted on different days, told her the same thing—she was interceding for a young girl having conflict with her parents.

I would imagine if there was a recording device during the day of Pentecost that would be awesome—many of us would understand those languages spoken by the upper room figures.

But you don't have to transcribe any uttered tongues unnecessarily unless you feel moved that it carries certain truths worth knowing. Understand that some of the unknown tongues are only gibberish expressions which cannot be related to any language on earth. When you record them no one would be able to interpret them unless God opens their understanding.

But if the speaking seems articulate and you feel curious to know what you are saying, write the expressions down or record them with your device.

However, I have come across people who have trained themselves to keep *rhema* words in their memories without easily forgetting them. Even the teachings and works of Jesus Christ were not written down during His time on earth, rather the disciples retained them in their memories through the help of the Holy Spirit and later wrote them down as we see today in the four Gospels and other epistles.

Transcribe any prompted thoughts, tongues, impressions and ideas down. Someone will help you to decode the meaning if you don't know.

INVESTIGATE PROMPTED UTTERANCES

We just learnt the importance of writing and recording *rhema* words received through praying. We gave the example of a lady who suspected she was speaking certain articulate languages but didn't know what it was until she consulted relevant sources to help interpret.

This reminds us of the dramatic announcement on May 26th 1961 by John F. Kennedy, the President of the United States of America, before a special Joint Session of Congress. The President informed the Congress about his ambition to send Americans to land on the moon.

On July 16th 1969 Apollo 11 blasted off into the air on its way to the moon. Neil Armstrong, Edwin "Buzz" Aldrin and Michael Collins were the first astronauts on board. Four days later, they landed on the moon and fixed the USA flag there while collecting stones and other particles to bring to earth. They were on the moon for three days and later came safely back to earth.

NASA's research and investigation turned that crazy hypothetical announcement into a new truth. Following that unbelievable venture, several orbit voyages to different planets took place.

Taking that into consideration, some utterances through tongues can lead us into certain truth we didn't know before. One time I was praying in tongues and kept on repeating the word "sycamore." I became conscious of what God was trying to tell me. I did investigate the "sycamore" word and found that it was the tree that Zacchaeus used to climb in order to clearly see Jesus. (Luke 19:4) I then understood what God was trying to convey to me to perfect my sight faculty.

If God has spoken to you using one of your five senses and you find it difficult to understand the message, investigate it using relevant sources.

However, if you go to believers who disagree about the validity of tongues, prophecies or healing you will surely be misled. Make use of mentors who have the same beliefs in the supernatural as you do.

Investigating from the Word

To be safe and on track we must always bring our inclinations subjective to the Word of God. The Bible tells us that, "Every word of God is pure: he is a shield unto them that put their trust in him." (Prov. 30:5) Similarly, in all occasions that you may be executing, "Do not add to His words, Lest He rebuke you, and you be found a liar." (v.6 NKJV) This should be your measuring rod in all your pursuit of knowledge.

The Prophet Daniel wanted to know the number of years and the circumstances surrounding the Babylonian captivity. He diligently searched the scroll written by the Prophet Jeremiah who was vocal about the captivity prophecies and thus Daniel became conversant with them. His investigation prompted him to pray and fast. He discovered a wide gap between God and Israel who were supposedly chosen as the flag bearer of the Light of God and yet disobeyed Him thus resulting in thier captivity. (Dan. 9:3-19)

The Prophet Habakkuk was shown the upcoming tragedy that would befall Israel and questioned God why unfairness was to happen. (Hab. 1:1-4) The Lord replied to Him but negatively—saying pagan nations would arise to destroy Israel. (v.5-11) Habakkuk became concerned and reasoned with God again why those who knew Him were to be humiliated by pagans who knew nothing about God. (v.12-17) After his reasoning prayer, he prepared himself ready to hear what God would say to prove him wrong. (Hab. 2:1)

God did speak to him ordering him to write the vision down for the future generation. 'Then the LORD answered me and said: "Write the vision And make *it* plain on tablets, That he may run who reads it."' (v.2)

These great men of faith understood the importance of investigating issues using the Word of God as well as praying. They knew the importance of the Word.

Similarly, what you talk in tongues can be investigated especially when it is believed to carry certain prophecies and symbols. Use the Bible as your first priority and then go back to pray the way Daniel and Habakkuk did.

God cannot show us something and leave us in confusion to decode the meaning by ourselves unnecessarily. In the earlier chapters, we did talk that speaking in tongues bypasses our mind and catches the devil off guard. The devil won't know what has been spoken. Your tongues answer may possibly be hidden in the Word. Check it out and if you are not sure go back to prayer again.

For example, you may be seeing fire as you are praying in tongues. The word "fire" in the Bible conveys several meanings and unless otherwise you do a thorough investigation in context to the atmospheric scene you observe while praying.

If you also received certain words you don't understand check the internet or books because they may be in Greek, Hebrew or other languages. Do a thorough search and your outcome should also be interpreted contextually in line with the scene.

Investigating from Experts

Janie Duvall prayed in a "suspicious" language and recorded it right away—just a three-minute recording. She decided to seek out language experts. She met several university professors in the United States to identify her tongues language.

All the professors identified that she was speaking a medieval language spoken in Europe, which astonished them all. One of the professors, a native Frenchman, said Janie was speaking an extinct language spoken by a Jewish French community living in *La Provincia* in France around 1300 A.D.

If she had not recorded and sought experts to identify and interpret the words for her, she would not have understood it and it would just look like gibberish.

Nehemiah investigated the status of Jerusalem from a right source—his own brother Hanani. (Neh. 1:2) Hanani told him, "The remnant that are left of the captivity there in the province are in great affliction and reproach: the wall of Jerusalem also is broken down, and the gates thereof are burned with fire." (v.3)

His investigation landed on the right source and resulted in a revolutionary action. Nehemiah was grieved, fasted and prayed for forgiveness and insight into what to do. (v.4-11) Through God's intervention the wall was rebuilt and the reproach was removed in Israel and security was restored. (Neh. 7:1-3)

Nehemiah did not investigate from the perspective of King Artaxerxes nor from the people who were negative to Israel. He enquired from Hanani who carried the same pain as Nehemiah. If you enquire about anointing from a spiritually blind person, two of you will catastrophically err and may ruin your life purposes. Thus Jesus says, "if the blind lead the blind, both shall fall into the ditch." (Matt. 15:14)

King Nebuchadnezzar had a disturbing dream but

refused to tell his "wise" but erratic confidants who claimed to be able to access deep matters in the spirit world. The astrologers, magicians, sorcerers and soothsayers had no way to understand. They said, "There is not a man on earth who can tell the king's matter." (Dan. 2:10) They were afraid and wanted the dream to be revealed by the King first before trying to interpret it. The King became furious because he realized that these soothsayers had misled him and the nation in many situations.

Daniel emerged to be a spiritual master and he attributed all glory to the Revealer. He prayed and God revealed the dream exactly by giving the interpretation and proper rendering. (v.17-23) It impelled the King to promote him and his friends to higher ranks. (v.46-49)

If you have some dreams, vision and utterances that seemed meaningful to you and you don't have the interpretation yet, find people who are mature, Spirit-filled and believe in the supernatural.

Caution! Always be careful with whom you consult. I have known many young believers who were desperate in spirit matters, but lost their vigor because they consulted the wrong Christians who cannot manage to pray even for more than ten minutes.

A few months ago, I was attending prayers in San Diego, California, and during prayer time the Lord revealed to me someone having pains in certain area of their body. I called the person to come forward for healing. After the service, she followed me outside wanting to know how I knew about her exact sickness. I told her when you pray especially with the spirit, God will reveal certain matters to you. The only thing is we have to be conscious about His voice and ways of transaction.

For example, a friend of mine told me they went to pray for a sick child in a hospital and the leading minister "prophesied" to the parents of the child that the child would live because God had told him. But few hours later the child died. Did that minister actually hear from God?

If you are a minister, enquiring about spiritual matters from Spirit-filled believers it doesn't make you less spiritual, especially if you are already a minister. God sometimes hides things from you and reveals them to others so that we all work together as one body. Even the Apostle Paul had Silas who was a prophet (Acts 15:32) to be with him as he ministered in different places. (v.40)

On several occasions Paul asked the church to pray for him so that God would open his mouth to speak the Word with boldness. (Eph. 6:19-20)

PART III

ACTIVATING TONGUES

CHAPTER 7

DESIRE TONGUES INTENSELY

Baptism in the Holy Spirit has been erroneously viewed with confusion and distortion by many. Such misconceptions have so far blocked many Christians from activating their tongues for the betterment of their lives and ministry. Even within those denominations that embrace tongues, many of their ministers have confusing views about when and how to receive the baptism in the Spirit. They teach wrong ways blocking the activation of tongues to others.

Many traditional denominations believe that when you are born again you are already baptized in the Holy Spirit and that there is no need for you to seek for the gift anymore—you have it already. Yet they don't even speak in tongues.

Others ministers believe in tongues but add more requirements. They say when you are born again you are actually baptized in the Holy Spirit, but you have to seek the infilling so that you will be able to speak in tongues and flow in the gifts of the Spirit. (1 Cor. 12)

However, some denominations teach that the baptism in the Holy Spirit with ability to speak in tongues was only for "certain" groups of believers who were chosen to carry special assignments that require a power and boldness. They use the early church as a typical example. The apostles ministered in hostile nations which demanded power and boldness. They claim if you try to seek for the gift and you don't receive, just relax; you are not part of the "special" chosen people.

Other denominations are more rigid. They reject the notion of baptism in the Holy Spirit as well as speaking in tongues. They believe tongues were only experienced in the early church when the New Testament was not yet written. Speaking in tongues is not operational today; it died together with the offices of apostles and prophets. We now live in a Bible period and everything we need concerning prophecies and tongues, can be found by reading the Bible. Any "outside" claimed experience is heretical.

However, the majority of charismatic denominations including "pockets" of believers within traditional churches believe the experience of regeneration during the salvation reception is quite different from baptism in the Holy Spirit. The Greek word **baptize,** where we find the word baptism means to immerse, to dip or to submerge.

In regeneration the Spirit of adoption to sonship comes in to quicken your *dead* spirit (which was dead because of sin) and makes it alive for eternal purposes. (Rom. 8:15) This does not mean you are actually filled in the Holy Spirit and are able to speak in tongues. Baptism in the Holy Spirit is for *ministry empowerment* not for eternal purposes. It deeply submerges one into the Spirit's chamber to retrieve enough power to minister the Word and withstand all odds attempting to hinder the work of the Gospel.

Before Jesus died on the Cross, the disciples were not born again. They were carnal. But after Jesus resurrected He appeared to the apostles and breathed a "quickening" Spirit into them to revive their spirits for eternal purposes—the salvation experience. (John 20:22) After that Jesus then gave them the Great Commission to fulfill. (Matt. 28:16-20) Nevertheless, He commanded them not to go out to preach yet. They must *wait* in Jerusalem until they were all baptized in the Holy Spirit to give them power and boldness to preach the Word of God. (Acts 1:4)

The Apostle Peter states clearly that the gift of the baptism in the Holy Spirit is not confined to one generation but to all generations until Christ comes again: "For the promise is unto you, and to your children, and to all that are afar off, even as many as the LORD our God shall call." (Acts 2:39)

Therefore, we must seek the gift with all diligence.

PRAYING TO RECEIVE TONGUES

When we were growing up some of my brothers would often request me to ask our father to grant them their desires. They knew if I asked him, that he would grant their desires rather than if they themselves asked him. They doubted their position of favor with our father.

I am sure my brothers did not have a clear understanding about how to approach our father and how they needed to adhere to the set principles our father expected. Our father wanted truth and clear reasons of what was desired especially if it was for noble purposes. He also wanted to see that what had been requested would be used accordingly.

But Jesus has given us a go-ahead to ask "whatsoever" we desire in our hearts. We should ask using His name and we will receive them. Jesus did not say ask what "He" desired you to have in order to receive but ask whatsoever "you" desire. (We will bold and italicize the verses for emphasis) Thus He says, "Therefore I tell you, ***whatever you ask*** in prayer, believe that you have received it, and it will be yours." (Mark 11:24 ESV)

What is that "whatever" Jesus is connoting here? Let's see this premise from a different angle.

In John 14: 13 Jesus said, "And ***whatsoever ye shall*** ask in my name, that will I do, that the Father may be glorified in the Son."

"If you abide in me, and my words abide in you, ***ask whatever you wish***, and it will be done for you." (John 15:7)

We must desire the ultimate gift for ministry to make us effective. Jesus commanded His disciples to wait until they were clothed with the power from above to enable them to perform incredible miracles. But the prerequisite for receiving the gift of tongues is to clear our mind from any negative distortion and revive it with faith.

We hear a lot of testimonies of people being baptized in the Holy Spirit while praying alone. It could happen during devotion time, at bed, during meditation while speaking verses to yourself. Sometimes you are worshipping God while singing. The only thing that matters is focus—I mean removing your mind from distraction and tuning it to God.

Another best moment to receive tongues is by the ministry of ministers. During such times people will easily catch up. We will explain this more later.

Vain Praying

Jesus cautions believers for abrogating the principle of asking to receive. The biggest weakness abrogating successful prayer is *disbelief*. Apostle James says, "But when you ask, *you must believe and not doubt*, because the one who doubts is like a wave of the sea, blown and tossed by the wind. That person should not expect to receive anything from the Lord." (James 1:6-7 emphasis italicized)

Usually disbelief is not openly spoken out but signs can tell us so and so's prayers are based on disbelief and doubt. Their prayers are concentrated with begging, pleading and complaining. If there is an onset of disbelief, doubts always sets in; we will begin doubting what scriptures speak about receiving and erroneously think God only grants what He wills.

This is one of the best doubting euphemisms we often confess: "I pray and I don't receive because maybe what I am asking is not according to God's will." The scripture that's most fallaciously quoted is 1 John 5:14 which says, "And this is the confidence that we have in him, that, if we ask anything according to his will, he heareth us."

But this scripture does not talk about "answering" of prayers rather it talks about God "hearing" your prayers. For example when I hear you talking or asking me for something it does not necessarily mean I have automatically answered you.

Some, even now, have not yet asked for the gift of tongues. They doubted what they have asked, which is not asking at all. They don't use the optimum protocol in asking. That is why Jesus rebuked the disciples to begin asking using his name. *"Until now you have not asked for anything in my name.* Ask and you will receive, and your joy will be complete." (John 16:24 NIV emphasis italicized)

Have you actually desired baptism in the Holy Spirit for so long and you feel you are sidelined and now left in limbo? Remember the desire of tongues is also included in the "whatsoevers" Jesus talks about. Never feel discouraged, just desire with *importunity* while developing your faith.

Jesus ascended to heaven after a period of about 40 days where he appeared to the disciples and confirmed He was alive. He also instructed them to wait in Jerusalem (and they chose the upper room) until they received the

Holy Spirit to clothe them with boldness and power for the ministry. (Acts 1:3-5)

From the Passover feast after Jesus was crucified to the feast of the Pentecost when the Holy Spirit came was 50 days. The disciples waited 10 days after Jesus' Ascension, praying and intensely seeking the promised gift. They didn't know when the Holy Spirit would arrive. They just waited by faith. Suddenly during the day of Pentecost as they were in one accord, the Holy Spirit came and baptized them all, and *they began* to speak in tongues vigorously. (Acts 2:1-4)

If the disciples were prepared to wait, constantly praying and seeking for the gift which they would finally receive, you can also spend your quality time seeking for the gift you desire. It is my prayer that if you have not yet activated your tongues, before finishing this book, you will soon be endowed with the power of the Holy Spirit to begin to speak in tongues.

Effective Praying

Cora Jakes Coleman, the daughter of Bishop TD Jakes wrote an interesting book entitled *Faithing It*. She tells of how she suffered from a polycystic ovarian syndrome causing infertility. Her doctors said she would never have children. The sickness humiliated her. Her dreams about having children and a family were shattered—her faith weakened.

Later, Cora understood that the power of faith supersedes all odds—I mean discouragements, despair and hopelessness. She started "faithing" her life again and hence received unfathomable peace, reviving all lost hopes. Cora is now happily married, having fostered children and eagerly expecting even more miracles to come her way. She has become a healing "mouth" to many young people who are despaired, heartbroken and have lost their faith.

There is power in faith. Faith can ignore, minimize and disregard all opposition and challenges coming from wherever. Paul says, *"But Scripture has locked up everything under the control of sin,* so that what was promised, *being given through faith in Jesus Christ,* might be given to those who believe."* (Gal. 3:22 NIV emphasis italicized)

The above text tells us that sin penetrates every part of our lives. God was prompted to secure our destined blessings in safe place thus awaiting sound faith to unlock them. The only key to unlock your desires— including tongues activation—is having faith in the promises of God. I mean a sound, doubtless faith. Such kind of faith eradicates disbelief and doubt.

The Bible talks about faith at length. Jesus revealed the breakthroughs of those coming to ask their desires from Him were the result of their faith and He commended their faith. (Matt. 8:9-11) The whole chapter of Hebrews 11 is dedicated to explain the power of faith which helped the biblical heroes to obtain the promises of God in their lives. They become known as "fathers of faith."

Scriptures assure us that the promises of the blessing of the Holy Spirit are for all. But they don't come by default; we have to unlock them by our faith through positive praying. "Truly I tell you, *if you have faith as small as a mustard seed*, you can say to this mountain, 'Move from here to there,' and it will move. Nothing will be impossible for you." (Matt. 17:20 NIV emphasis italicized)

If your faith about speaking in tongues is watered down due to erroneous teachings and failures, you still have a chance. Revive it. Your faith could be as small as a mustard seed yet it will work for you.

In the preceding chapters I wrote about a believer in the USA who felt he never heard God speaking to him audibly. He read my other book entitled *Power* and began to seek God ardently to experience Him. He even took three days off from work. His case was resolved; he encountered God in a more profound way which opted him to testify before his church.

Let your faith grow in every area with respect to your destiny. If you do so, nothing will hinder you; your prayers will receive tremendous results.

SEEKING TO RECEIVE TONGUES

Saul was seeking to find the lost donkeys of his father, Kish, and he travelled along with their family servant to different places and reached the place where Prophet Samuel was residing. In the process of seeking their lost donkeys they met the Seer and received prophetic words which bewildered Saul. (1 Sam. 9: 19-21) Saul was anointed by Samuel and the Holy Spirit descended on him on the way, and he began to prophesy thus surprised those watching the procession of prophets. (1 Sam.10: 9-11)

As you continue to seek the gift of tongues, you will find yourself "stumbling" upon more blessings you never expected. People will be surprised about you as they were with Saul. They will wonder whether you are "among the prophets."

Bishop TD Jakes tells of how he stumbled on a land full of rich minerals. As a family, they prayed for God to locate for them an area where they would buy a house. Indeed, God located a certain place and they bought a house there. Just sixty days later, mineral engineers tested the area and discovered natural gas underneath the ground. They paid them huge sums of money for both the land and their houses.

If you commit your ways to the Lord and desire tongues, you will definitely stumble on the gift of tongues unexpectedly with bonuses too. Just "Commit to the LORD whatever you do, and he will establish your plans." (Pr. 16:3 NIV)

Burning desire urges you to seek all possible ways to meet your desired needs. If you are required to travel to seek help from others, don't hesitate. The intensity will keep burning inside until it is fulfilled. Saturate your mind with faith building passages and surround yourself with faith uplifting people who are open to help you succeed.

Since childhood, I had desired to go to Israel to see with my eyes the events and locations spoken in the Word of God. I put in my heart that when I went there, God would bless me remarkably. He did. Recently I was in Israel to co-facilitate a conference combining Christians, Messianic and Orthodox Jews. And yes, I saw many of the locations mentioned in the Bible.

How did it happen? It was through intense desire and faith. The book you are reading is the result of my encounter with the Lord in Jerusalem.

Importuning Seeking

Importunity is defined as a persistent, insisting desire about something without giving up, no matter what it would cost. Importunity prompts a burning desire with a compelling force. It costs you to do anything possible to make you achieve what you want to have. It costs your energy, emotions and will, thus helping you devise ways to aid the achievement.

We read the story of a Canaanite woman importuning Jesus Christ to deliver her daughter vexed by evil spirits. Her shameless audacity annoyed the disciples of Jesus but "forced" Jesus to reason with her prophetically. Initially Jesus was reluctant and told her the time for Gentiles was not yet come; His mission was first to the house of Jacob. But her desire was intensified even more thus compelled Jesus Christ to grant her wishes. (Matt. 15:21-28)

If the Canaanite woman, who was not a believer, could compel Jesus to act on her wishes at an inappropriate time, what about you who has received Jesus Christ as Lord and Savior? Do you really desire the infilling of the Holy Spirit so that you will be able to speak in tongues? Do you want to operate supernaturally to the standard you are made to reach?

(Mark 16:17-18) Simply, just desire the gift.

As the desire for the gift intensifies, you may if necessary, have to venture into serious commitment through prayer and fasting. My book on *Power* explains in details some of the ultimate ways to effective praying. I would highly recommend you to find and read it.

When Daniel desired God to give Him an answer about the captivity and the number of years, he did two things: he studied the writings of Prophet Jeremiah and then prayed. He wanted to have a solid ground about the captivity narrated by Prophet Jeremiah so that his prayers would be on point. He then "prayed earnestly to the Lord God, pleading with him, fasting, wearing sackcloth, and sitting in ashes." (Dan. 9:2-3)

Ignorant praying is a stumbling block to answered prayers. We sometimes pray erroneously and because of that, the fruit of our prayers is not seen at all. If you are ignorant of tongues, then seeking God with a focus becomes so difficult.

Without intense desire to know God, lack of knowledge is evidenced. The desires of Daniel to know details about the captivity helped him streamline his prayers optimally— not in ambiguity like many of us often do. In fact, speaking in tongues is very important because it helps us pray in the Spirit according to God's intent and on precision.

Communal Seeking

I know sometimes when we seek the gift of the Holy Spirit by praying, we receive. However sometimes we don't. We need others to stand with us and help us. There is evidence in the Bible where many believers were helped by others to receive the infilling of the Holy Spirit.

For example, when Paul was struck with blindness on his way to Damascus to arrest Christians, God sent a certain disciple called Ananias to lay hands on him in order to open his eyes and be filled with the Holy Spirit as well as get baptized in water. (Acts 9:15-19)

Similarly, Cornelius, the captain of the Roman soldiers sought the presence of the Apostle Peter to help him and his family learn how to embrace the Lord. Peter came and before he finished preaching, the Holy Spirit fell on them and they began to speak with other tongues. Tongues proved to the Jews that the Romans had also been saved which compelled Peter to boldly order them to be baptized in water. (Acts 10:44-48)

The Apostle Paul came to Ephesus to strengthen the

believers there and realized they were not baptized in the Holy Spirit. So Paul laid his "hands upon them, the Holy Ghost came on them; and they spake with tongues, and prophesied." (Acts 19:6)

In another context, Peter and John were sent to Samaria to help those who believed in Christ through the ministry of the Evangelist Phillip. When they came they realized the believers were born again but hadn't received the baptism of the Holy Spirit. "Then laid they their hands on them, and they received the Holy Ghost." (Acts 8:17)

We have heard a number of believers who testify of getting air tickets to go to impartation conferences for the purpose of tongues. They had tried to receive the Holy Spirit by themselves but nothing happened until they were prayed for by other ministers.

You might have tried to seek the gift of tongues privately but with no results; God may be teaching you faith—He wants you to take a step of faith which would even cost your finances just to meet someone to help you in this particular matter.

This also teaches that we are one and need each other especially in the divine common work of God.

My seminary professor once told us that he sought

to receive the gift of tongues but to no avail. He felt disappointed and gave up—thinking the gift was for a specific group of believers other than him. So one time he was walking the streets of New York City and unexpectedly met his Russian school mates. They asked him whether he was baptized in the Holy Spirit or not. He told them he was still skeptical.

They encouraged him to believe by faith and they would love to pray for him. He did believe and knelt on the sidewalk expecting the gift. His friends laid hands on him and instantly power came upon him and he began to speak in tongues praising God.

Do you feel disappointed that you have failed to receive what you desire from God, not only the gift of tongues but other gifts as well? If Jesus, despite the Jewish customs prohibiting them from associating with Gentiles, was able to grant the Canaanite woman her request because of her great faith, then you are not an exception. You, even more than the Canaanite woman are liable to receive, because Jesus has redeemed you on the Cross. Strengthen your faith and strive for excellence.

I proclaim Isaiah 60:1 to your life to "Arise, shine; for thy light is come, and the glory of the LORD is risen upon thee." It's never too late for you. Just prepare yourself to be ready for your miracles.

CHAPTER 8

SPEAK PROMPTED UTTERANCES

We are now reaching to the tactical ways that would easily help you speak in tongues. These proven ways come through experience as well as descriptions in the scriptures.

I remember one time a friend of mine tried to fix some jets in a manufacturing company. It took him longer and yet he failed to fix them. His method was wrong, demanding much effort for what could have been an easy fix.

When I came in, I found him struggling. I took him aside and told him to watch the way I would do it. Within a few minutes I had fixed the problem.

The reason he failed to fix the problem was because he didn't follow the rules prescribed in the manual.

Have you ever missed finding a place where you want to go to, and find yourself wandering around the streets where you become a hazard to drivers? It's not that the place is difficult to find, it's just that you might have ignored or missed the posted signs directing people accordingly. God has given us very concise ways that would easily help us receive the gift of tongues. We have to be keen in studying the movement of the Holy Spirit during prayer moments. If we train ourselves, we will be able to recognize the presence of God and embrace Him for our good.

The believers were in one accord awaiting the gift Jesus promised them. That accord is a bonding connection for the awaited gift. The Spirit of the Lord descended on each one of them, filled them up and gave them utterances. They cooperated by speaking those prompted utterances.

They did not wait for the Spirit to speak in them but they spoke out the prompts which resulted in uttering diverse languages. "And they were all filled with the Holy Ghost, and began to speak with other tongues, as the Spirit gave them utterance." (Acts 2:4)

One time, we were praying for a lady who was desiring to speak in tongues. The power of God touched her and she reported certain prompts within her but she closed her mouth, waiting for the Holy Spirit to speak in her. Guess what! She failed to receive the gift at that moment.

After a while, I told her she should open her heart and release any prompted utterance. She did and instantly spoke in tongues for the first time. She would usually pray for less than ten minutes, but that time she spoke in tongues for more than two hours.

We also have to be aware that some people testify of receiving the gift of tongues without feeling any urges. Ministers encouraged them to begin speaking tongue languages and they did.

One of them was Sid Roth of *Its Supernatural.* He narrated on his TV program that when he received tongues, he didn't feel anything. He even doubted if he received tongues and the Holy Spirit was helping him out. It was not until his mother one time was astonished how he was able to speak fluent ancient Hebrew. On another occasion, he also spoke in tongues and his adherents were amazed wondering how he knew the Filipino dialect. From thereon, he realized he was "actually" baptized in the Holy Spirit.

We cannot fathom the operations of God in His people. He works in mysterious ways. When I first spoke in tongues in my younger years, I had no idea about what I was doing. No one ever told me it was called "speaking in tongues." I used to speak to my friends in tongues and we would make fun of it. One time my mother reproved me for acting in such a weird manner. I told her I was coining a language similar to my mother tongue. I told her one time many of them would speak the language I was speaking. Later I realized that this was a prophecy. It's true, today speaking in tongues is gaining more momentum than ever before.

The gift of tongues comes in a variety of ways. Many people report receiving the gift through personal devotion or singing, while others receive it through impartation prayers, through the laying on of hands or declaring the Word.

Let's now study some of the phenomena of the gift of tongues and explain easy ways to receive the gift or impart to others.

GROUNDBREAKING FOR TONGUES ACTIVATION

When a person wants to build a house, he sits down to plan how, where, when and what to do in regards to the building project. After planning and making sure human and material resources are available, there has to be a groundbreaking for the project to start. The foundation of the house has to be properly constructed to make the house stand strong. When earthquakes and tornadoes knock against the house it will remain strong and steady. (Luke 6:46-49)

Have you ever taken time to study the phenomenon of tongues using scriptures and listening to those who have experienced the gift? In fact, God takes into consideration those who are prepared before blessing them. Truly, He encourages preparation in believers despite what level their spiritual stamina would be.

Before the day of Pentecost, Jesus commanded the disciples to tarry in one place to prepare themselves for the gift. They were preparing themselves, probably studying scriptures—we see Peter quoting scripture about Judas Iscariot's replacement—and all devoted themselves to prayers. (Acts 1:14, 16) The Holy Spirit came into a "prepared" heart. (Acts 2:1-4)

Compare the two prophetic comments Peter made before they were filled in the Holy Spirit and after receiving the Holy Spirit. They chose a replacement for Judas Iscariot by casting *lots* as practiced by priests those days. (Acts 1:26; Luke 1:9) They were not able to hear God *within*. But after the Pentecost day, the church did not use lot casting; rather they used the gifts of the Spirit to choose men full of faith and Holy Ghost to be deacons. The men were presented before the apostles for ordination through laying of hands. (Acts 6:6)

You may have been seeking the gift of the Spirit for some time; God is actually preparing you for greater miracles. Take time to study all trends of tongues if you can and hear what the Lord is saying to you. This practice will make your faith ready for supernatural intervention. Romans 10:17 says, "So then faith comes by hearing, and hearing the word of God." This "hearing" can include of course, studying the Word and hearing what it says as you mediate upon it.

Reflect on the phenomenon at Cornelius' house: "While Peter yet spake these words, the Holy Ghost fell on all them which heard the word." (Acts 10:44) They heard the word of God from Peter and their faith grew to a threshold of miracles and they received the gift of tongues.

Hearing the Word of God develops great desire for the gift. But hearing negative words, attacking what you desire, will kill your faith. Many people left Christianity because of negative association with faith attackers.

Seek out scriptures that inspire your faith for tongues. You cannot become a medical doctor while studying business administration.

Desire the gift. Look at the parable Jesus gave about the friend who came at night asking for bread to give his visitor. (Luke 11:5-7) The friend was reluctant to rise up from bed, "yet because of his importunity he will rise and give him as many as he needeth." (v.8) That "importunity" is an insisting desire.

Jacob refused to leave the angel fighting him until he was blessed. (Gen. 32:26) The Apostles including all the 120 delegates refused to leave the upper room until they received the Promise of the Father. Have you ever desired for the gift of tongues with importunity? If so, have you received the gift and are you able to understand how the Holy Spirit speaks to you?

Worship is a good groundbreaking, preparing believers to receive the Holy Spirit. When we enter into deep worship, we "switch off" from the natural and "walk" in the spirit realm. We will find it easy to decode any message placed in our inner beings. At that moment, any request you make will definitely be whisked away by angels for deliberation at the throne of Grace. (Rev. 8:3)

If you desire to speak in tongues, tell Jesus at that moment because He is the Baptizer in the Spirit. His name opens the doors of heaven to make your requests reach the throne of God. For John says, "I baptize you with water for repentance. But after me comes one who is more powerful than I, whose sandals I am not worthy to carry. *He will baptize you with the Holy Spirit and fire.*" (Matt. 3:11 NIV emphasis italicized)

Another groundbreaking practice is fasting. Fasting is simply saying no to the distraction of food and other practices and saying yes to God by giving your precious time to seek His presence. It helps in making us find enough time to focus on God. We discipline our busy stomach to rest. Doctors reveal that fasting improves health. In fasting we give chance for the body to rest—I mean the digestive glands hibernate for a while thus prompting recovery.

Impartation sessions are also pivotal to receiving the gift of tongues. The reason is many "crazy" Holy Spirit seekers have already invited the *manifest* presence of God into the place. When you enter into such a ground, the power of God will easily overshadow you. When Cornelius was praying alone, God heard him and spoke to him but he was not filled in the Holy Spirit. But the presence of Peter, a Spirit-filled man drenched the atmosphere with the Holy Ghost. He was yet speaking and the Holy Spirit fell on the Gentiles and they began to speak in tongues. (Acts 10:44)

This reminds me of the time I went to Kansas City for a conference. Several Spirit-filled believers went to the conference hall early just to declare the manifest presence of God. When the service began the power of God was vividly manifested and many people received amazing miracles which they had been seeking for long time.

However, I have also attended some prayer meetings where no manifested glory of God was seen. Everything in the service was dry, including singing and preaching. No one even responded to altar calls. Prayer was given a small amount of time and replaced with more extra communal stuff, which is sad.

DYNAMICS OF TONGUES ACTIVATION

Today, there are different assumptions focusing on the occurrences during tongues activation. Several practices have been noticed within the charismatic movements trying to help activate tongues in believers. Some of the methods they teach or practice have actually confused the processes thus prompting critics to challenge the gift using different arguments.

Some critics argue that the act of speaking gibberish tongues is just coined by ludicrous ministers who pretend as if they have secrets into the spirit world while hypnosis is cleverly devised. They claim when people are "slain" in the power of the Holy Spirit, as it's claimed, it is actually a hypnotic mind wandering, making people dizzy and hence they fall to the ground.

Others see speaking in tongues as devilish and warn adherents to shun the phenomenon of tongues as a whole. What if the Holy Spirit operates all these trends? How would we cope with the warnings from Jesus Himself? "Therefore I say unto you, All manner of sin and blasphemy shall be forgiven unto men: *but the blasphemy against the Holy Spirit shall not be forgiven* unto men." (Matt. 12:31 emphasis italicized)

On the other hand, I want to bring into focus some of the experiential practices to activate tongues using biblical methods seen in the book of Acts when the Holy Spirit descended on the first recipients of tongues. We will bold and italicize some verse phrases for emphasis.

Tongues Activation in Acts

In order to receive the gift of tongues there must be desire and waiting upon the Lord with eagerness. Jesus even uses a "tarrying" command to enlighten us about the importance of *waiting*. He didn't want the disciples to go preach without supernatural clothing. He "commanded them that they should not depart from Jerusalem, **but wait** *for the promise of the Father, which,* saith he, ye have heard of me." (Acts 1:4)

The baptism of the Holy Spirit is revealed as a "power" for witnessing the Gospel: "But *ye shall* **receive power***, after that the Holy Ghost is come upon you: and ye shall* **be witnesses** *unto me* both in Jerusalem, and in all Judaea, and in Samaria, and unto the uttermost part of the earth." (v.8)

"And when the day of Pentecost was fully come, they *were all with* **one accord** *in one place.* And suddenly there came a sound from heaven as of *a rushing mighty wind, and it filled all the house where they were sitting.* And there appeared unto them cloven tongues like as of fire, and it sat upon each of them. And *they were all* **filled** *with the Holy Ghost, and* **began** *to speak with other tongues, as* **the Spirit gave them utterance."** (Acts 2:1-4)

The second group of the people to receive tongues *first believed in Jesus Christ*, got baptized in Jesus' name and then were filled with the Holy Spirit: "Then Peter said unto them, **Repent**, and **be baptized** every one of you in the name of Jesus Christ for the remission of sins, and **ye shall receive the gift** *of the Holy Ghost.*" (v.38)

Another trend of *laying on of hands* to receive the Holy Spirit is practiced here. Ananias did lay hands on Saul (who became Paul) to receive the gift: "And Ananias went his way, and entered into the house; and **putting his hands on him** *said*, Brother Saul, the Lord, even Jesus, that appeared unto thee in the way as thou camest, hath sent me, that thou mightest receive thy sight, and **be filled with the Holy Ghost.**" (Acts 4:31)

Peter and John were sent to Samaria where Phillip converted many people to Christ. They believed, but were not filled in the Holy Spirit. So Peter and John used their hands to impart the Holy Ghost on them: "Then **laid they their hands on them**, and **they received the Holy Ghost**." (Acts 8:17)

Again the Holy Spirit is said to have "fallen" unexpectedly on Gentiles while Peter was preaching the Gospel: "While Peter yet spake these words, *the Holy*

*Ghost **fell on all them** which heard the word... For **they heard them speak with tongues,** and magnify God."* (Acts 10:44, 46)

The eloquent Apollos was in Ephesus where his preaching resulted in many people converting to the Lord, but he didn't do anything concerning the baptism of the Holy Spirit, for he only knew John's baptism. (Acts 18:24-25) Paul came there and realized the believers were not baptized in the Holy Spirit: "And when **Paul had laid his hands upon them, the Holy Ghost came on them; and they spake with tongues,** and prophesied." (Acts 19:6)

Looking at the above passages we find the Holy Spirit baptizing believers using diverse ways: During preaching time (of course by Spirit-filled ministers), the Holy Spirit would fall on people unexpectedly. Sometimes the Holy Spirit would baptize people as they were in one accord praying for the gift with high expectation, as well as by laying on of hands.

Those who received the gift did not use mechanical ways to speak in tongues. Rather they were filled in the Holy Spirit and were given divine utterances. They *cooperated* by speaking out the given utterances in which we call "speaking in tongues."

Faults in Tongues Activation

I recently tried to start my car engine but it didn't work. I tried once more, but all in vain. After careful examination, I realized I was using a wrong key. When I picked the right key, pushed it into the ignition area and turned the key, the engine worked perfectly.

I later compared the two types of keys. Both were used for Toyota cars but each had a slight difference.

Like the car key, many people have not activated their gift of tongues because those teaching them used wrong methods.

Some ministers teach believers to get baptized in the Holy Spirit by mimicking others. They start by speaking one or two gibberish words and asking tongues-seeking students to mimic them. After the students master few gibberish sentences, they are then encouraged to coin their own words or mimic other speakers. These students are encouraged to continue mimicking until they are fluent in "tongues."

Yes, we know God understands our ignorance and sometimes uses His grace to help us get filled in the Holy Spirit even though we are at fault. But that should not be taken as "another" proven way for tongues.

The irony is that these students who are now deemed

as "Spirit filled" don't have the inner conviction and assurance they are filled or baptized in the Holy Spirit. They don't believe their speaking in tongues is speaking in divine languages. Any person challenging them slightly about tongues will trample their faith because their faith anchoring is distorted.

I watched a pastor on the Internet challenging that speaking in tongues was unreal. He told how his former pastor from a Pentecostal denomination told them to mimic tongues. They did and were congratulated for being filled. But inside him was a great hollow—doubt. Later a Seventh Day Adventist (SDA) member preached to him and refuted the Charismatic movement's notion as emotional and unbiblical. It opened his eyes and he has now switched to the SDA.

Another similar method is where ministers tell people to start speaking in tongues using whatever words would come from their mouth. They should not think of making a mistake, but just speak. The more they speak, the more they are exerting the power of the Holy Spirit within them.

I know of some people who actually got filled in the

Holy Spirit by just beginning to speak in tongues. A well-known pastor testified that when he was a young believer, his pastor encouraged him to start speaking in tongues using any random words. He didn't feel any prompts but later realized he got filled in the Holy Spirit.

Yes, that trend may work because we know God understands our weakness but the atmosphere has to be prepared first. People have to be expectant to receive anything from the Lord.

Unusual Occurrences in Tongues Activation

There is power when a person is baptized in the Holy Spirit. People who are *actually* baptized in the power of the Holy Spirit cannot yield to other falsifications about tongues to discredit the trend. They have experienced certain experiences in their bodies that cannot be denied. They also have a credible assurance about their salvation because of the divine experiences.

For example, when I was on my way to Canada, I met some university students in Uganda and one of them tried to "educate" me that "Canada was a province of the United States and its president was George W. Bush." He tried to convince me by bragging he was a university student in the Faculty of Education.

I later told him I had already gotten my visa and within three days I would be flying to Canada. I also had a booklet introducing Canada as an independent country unique from the United States of America. I had already met Canadian embassy officials and I knew where I was going to live, including my house address. He could attempt to deceive other people but not me.

If you have a personal experience of the infilling of the Holy Spirit, you are safe from confusion because you have a personal encounter which is unexplainable.

When the Spirit of God overshadows a believer, the Spirit's power overpowers the person. There are moments people begin to fall down in the power of the Holy Spirit even though they struggle to stand. A tall lady, who used to challenge those people who were falling where the pastors were assumed to be pushing people down, fell during prayers and remained down for over five minutes. The pastor did not actually touch her during prayer but rather raised his hand toward her. When she woke up, those people whom she had criticized began to tease her for falling. She now believes the power of the Spirit is real. (Note also that some ministers tend to push people down to impress others.)

Some believers do shake and feel some moving "electricity" inside them. Others begin laughing uncontrollably, a practice which is receiving a lot of criticism.

Other believers, when they get baptized in the Spirit, begin to babble some weird words. Any uninformed person might feel something wrong is happening.

Some Christians begin articulating statements using languages that are understandable. They themselves may not know what they are speaking but those around would hear them speaking articulate languages.

Let's now see how the first apostles got baptized in the Holy Spirit. This would be followed by their consecutive infillings and later by newcomers' baptisms in the Spirit. We will italicize and bold those areas of our concern.

BLOCKAGES IN TONGUES ACTIVATION

There was a time our kitchen sink was filled with dirty water. We tried several ways to pump air to remove what was blocking the drain but all efforts failed. We finally had to call a plumber who managed to remove a big stuff blocking the water from flowing through the pipe.

Using air pressure was not working as it pushed the blockage further down the pipe. After removing the blockage, the plumber cleared the pipe and everything became functional again.

Similarly when you really desire tongues and you feel you haven't received yet, be mindful that there is something wrong blocking you from accessing the gift. Don't be frustrated, rather find out the blockage and remove it so that the desired gift would be ushered in.

I am reminded of a story of two crippled South African friends, one of them heard the news that a healing evangelist was in town conducting a crusade. He went to get his friend so that they would go to attend but his friend refused. He pleaded with him to accompany him even though he had no interest. His friend later agreed and they came to the meeting place.

The evangelist prayed for healing and his friend, who initially refused to come, got healed while he was not.

During testimony time the evangelist asked anyone who accompanied the healed crippled person to come forward and to verify the healing. He came forward in a wheel chair, not healed. He thanked God for healing his colleague. The evangelist then asked him, "Two of you were crippled and you came with your friend here and he is now healed while you are not. How do you feel and actually what blocked you from receiving your own healing?"

If you put yourself into the situation of that unhealed crippled man, how would you feel and what would you conclude about your fate?

Speaking frankly, there are numerous blockages hindering the manifestation of the Holy Spirit in our lives. Many people who desire to experience the baptism of the Holy Spirit have made every effort but have failed to receive. They are left in a dilemma. Those who are baptized in the Holy Spirit live a "dry" life devoid of divine manifestation—dunamis. There is no difference between a Spirit-filled believer and professing Christian. What is going on?

Here comes the question: Are you convinced *within* that you are baptized in the Holy Spirit and are able to speak in tongues? If your answer is yes, then I have another question: Are you currently ministering to others to receive the gift of the Spirit and do they receive the gift as you minister? If not, then something somewhere is wrong and needs rectification. I want to highlight some of the blockages preventing us from accessing the miraculous works of the Spirit.

One of the major problems which prevents receiving tongues activation is *sin*. The Bible tells us that sin hinders us from seeing the face of the Lord and blocks our blessings: "But your ***iniquities*** have separated you from your God; And your ***sins*** have hidden His face from you, So that ***He will not hear.*** " (Isa. 59:2)

If sin can hide the face of the Lord from us, then our prayers are already amiss. What we desire and pray about doesn't reach the throne of God. The sin, not God, has blocked the access. Your prayers only hit the wall— the wall is sin itself.

The other blockage is *blaspheming* of the Holy Spirit. The Father was overt in the Old Testament period; Jesus became overt too when He was on earth. He finished His saving mission on earth and is in heaven busy preparing rooms for us. He left His name for us to use to access divine stuff.

But when He ascended to heaven He sent the Holy Spirit on earth to be "another" comforter with us and so to live inside us and fill us with power.

Nevertheless, many Christians including some ministers reject and blaspheme Him every day and moment. How can He fill you up and work in you when you hate Him? For example, if you reject me and always challenge my works how can I trust you and delegate you to do some of my noble works? I don't think so. Jesus asserts in Mark 3:29-30 that *"'he who blasphemes against the Holy Spirit never has forgiveness,* but is subject to eternal condemnation"—because they said, "He has an unclean spirit."'

Blaspheming the Holy Spirit is an act of speaking profane words against God and His acts. Jesus was performing miracles in the power of the Holy Spirit but the Pharisees attributed the Spirit's works to an unclean spirit. They discredited the manifestation of the Holy Spirit. Jesus calls the sin of blasphemy *unforgiven* because it is actually rejecting the Person who works to connect you with God and seals you up. (Eph. 1:13) It's just like rejecting a pilot while expecting the plane to fly you over to Hawaii.

We see many ministers of God performing amazing miracles in the power of the Holy Spirit who are referred to as satanic. Pray for discernment to enable you distinguish how satan operates and how God operates too. Don't just use mental guessing. Yes, I know there are multitude of satanic agents disguising as sheep but their fruit can be seen. We should not discredit other people because the miracles they perform are beyond our imagination rather let's correct them with acts that counteract the biblical norms.

When Jesus ascended to heaven He handed the *charge* to the Holy Spirit. (John 14:16) If you reject or talk against the Holy Spirit, you are actually rejecting the Father and the Son including the ministration of angels. You may try to receive the infilling of the Spirit but…. Just finish this phrase yourself.

Furthermore, *denominational barriers* are blockages hindering the Holy Spirit from working in us. If you go against the doctrine of your denomination, even though what you are practicing is biblical you are already in error, thus you are reprimanded. These hurdles cause fear and delusion among Christians.

Sometimes those who are desiring the gift are the problem themselves. During prayer time, which is important for divine impartation, they however focus their mind on people or their own status instead of focusing on God. Some of them may be thinking, "Oh someone is watching me. I don't want to act foolish." They lose focus and distance themselves from receiving the gift of tongues.

Others have a mind that wanders all over during

prayer moments. Even though they come forward for prayer their mind is thinking things that are contrary to God—evil thoughts.

Some respondents refuse to speak "urges" of the Holy Spirit. They don't corporate with the Holy Spirit at all. Acts 2:7 reveals how the apostles cooperated with God. The Holy Spirit overshadowed them, gave them utterances and they spoke out those utterances. They did not close their mouths awaiting the Holy Spirit to open and speak through them. No, they worked side by side.

The Bible tells us in Joel 2:28-29 that at the latter days— meaning the church age where we are right now, "And it shall come to pass afterward, that I will pour out my spirit upon all flesh; and your sons and your daughters shall prophesy, your old men shall dream dreams, your young men shall see visions: And also upon the servants and upon the handmaids in those days will I pour out my spirit."

CHAPTER 9

EXERCISE TONGUES REGULARLY

There is a saying that practice makes perfect. People who fear practicing always lose. They fear because they doubt what they already have. Doubt stems from the mind thus blocking the normal operation of the inner being. It does not see possibilities but impossibilities.

Doubt tosses doubters "like a wave of the sea that is driven and tossed by the wind. (James 1:6 ESV)

Just see the mood of people in church when they see a physical miracle being performed. Everybody becomes so expectant. At that moment, when they are called forward for prayer, the altar will be full of desperate people ready to expect miracles. Jesus says, "Except ye see signs and wonders, ye will not believe." (John 4:48)

When we want people to respond for their salvation, healing, deliverance during preaching, we have to prepare them to reduce the level of doubt while raising their belief to a threshold for miracles.

"If thou canst believe, all things are possible to him that believeth." (Mark 9:23)

Praying in tongues helps prepare the ground for the supernatural. In fact, you might experience "strange" encounters as you go on praying. When you sense, see, hear or receive a word in your spirit, act it out if need be. Jesus says, "He can do only what *he sees his Father doing.*" (John 5:19 NIV emphasis italicized)

Moses did not know that he had the anointing (staff) of God in his hand until he was told to act upon it. He was shocked and fled from the staff he usually carried. "And God said, 'Cast it on the ground.' And he cast it on the ground, and it became a serpent; and Moses fled from before it." (Ex. 4:3)

The disciples of Jesus didn't realize what they had until they went into the field where God performed amazing miracles through them. "And the seventy returned again with joy, saying, Lord, even the devils are subject unto us through thy name." (Luke 10:17)

The church that prayed at the house of the mother of John Mark didn't believe their prayers would release Peter from the prison. Peter "came to the house of Mary the mother of John, whose surname was Mark; where many were gathered together praying.... But Peter continued knocking: and when they had opened the door, and saw him, *they were astonished.*" (Acts 12:12, 16 emphasis italicized)

We should not give the devil a chance to continue whispering to us so that we don't fulfill the purposes of God in our lives. Pray in tongues so that your words will bypass the devil as well as your mind. As you go on praying, if you receive some words, impressions or inclinations don't be afraid to act them out. You will be stunned to see tumultuous results.

The young Timothy was ordained a pastor by Paul and had manifested certain gifts useful for his office. But he was shying away from performing his pastoral duty. Paul, as his spiritual father, had to encourage him to move forward. "For this reason I remind you to fan into flame the gift of God, which is in you through the laying on of my hands." (2 Tim. 1:6 NIV)

Don't be intimidated that you will err in your spiritual pursuit—yes you will err but that should not bog you down. Mistakes are not meant for condemnation. All of us have made some mistakes or blunders in certain areas. Even the Prophet Elijah tried to "educate" God saying he was the only true prophet left in Israel and was being hunted by Jezebel.

(1 Kings 19:10) But God corrected him saying, "I have reserved seven thousand in Israel, all whose knees have not bowed to Baal, and every mouth that has not kissed him." (v.18 NKJV)

Thomas Edson, the inventor of electric light attempted his innovation for over one thousand times and all in vain. His critics lauded his failure in order to discourage him. When Thomas was interviewed by his associate, Walter L. Mallory, he refused to call it a failure or even a mistake. Instead he talked of finding a thousand theories that wouldn't work in the invention of the electric light. Afterwards he succeeded in his invention.

You should not do things just to try. Take the word "trying' out from your mind. Declare you are going to make it by the grace of God and you will do as you prophesy to yourself.

Remember "Unto whomsoever much is given, of him shall be much required: and to whom men have committed much, of him they will ask the more" (Luke 12:48) and so, speaking in tongues as well as tongues interpretation is not an exception. All these are gifts from God they must be exercised maximally.

REGULARIZING TONGUES SPEAKING

Any regular exercise we continue will make a great difference in our lives. In school, for example, when a student ignores taking classes as mandated and doesn't study nor does homework, passing exams becomes just a dream. If you want to build strong muscles, you must do regular exercise using prescribed principles as per your requirements. Everything we do regularly pays dividends.

Similarly, exercising tongues regularly is a strong edification for our spiritual stamina. The Bible assures us that when believers pray in tongues, even though not interpreted they edify themselves. The Apostle Paul managed to take the Gospel to emperors, kings and different personalities around the ancient world because he empowered himself through regular praying. He says, "I thank God that I speak in tongues more than all of you." (1 Cor. 14:18 NIV)

Oral Roberts said his successful founding and sustenance of Oral Roberts University was due to his much speaking in tongues. He admitted he would speak in tongues at least ten times a day and with interpretation too. God would direct him to guide the University accordingly.

Supernatural Positioning

A renowned minister of God was once interviewed by secular journalists and pressed on certain distractive questions in an attempt to turn him into an ordinary preacher. He refused to answer those questions. This is what he told the journalists: "I am not 'just' a preacher but a man of God." I hope the interviewers understood what he was trying to explain.

That man knew he carried power from above and his preaching was not a religious kind of talking. He knew his preaching was concentrated with power from above. Ordinary preaching is merely a blending of human techniques just to impress others without spending time in concentrated prayer.

Paul says, "My speech and my preaching was not with enticing words of man's wisdom, but in demonstration of the Spirit and of power." (1 Cor. 2:4)

Paul's supposition is proven in Acts 19:12 that, from his "...body were brought unto the sick handkerchiefs or aprons, and the diseases departed from them, and the evil spirits went out of them."

Where and how did that power come from where anything touching Paul's body was able to heal and deliver people? Which principle did Paul actually use enabling him to walk in such a mighty power? Let's see some of his revealed secrets:

"I thank my God, I speak with tongues more than ye all." (1 Cor. 14:18) Paul reveals here that he spends regular times speaking in tongues to edify himself, soak his words and body with dunamis—power from above. In facts in Acts 17:18, his critics call him a "babbler," typifying his strange utterances. Could it be tongues?

If you are a Spirit-filled believer, speak in tongues regularly especially in your private praying. Many amazing miracles will happen in your life.

Today we have ministers of God who spend quality time praying in tongues and God is using them greatly. The manifestation of the power of God is vividly seen in their meetings and some stunned people begin attributing their demonstration to Beelzebub. (Matt. 12:24) They find it difficult to understand.

The more you spend time praying in the Spirit, the clearer you will hear the voice of God. You are actually "expanding" your inner man in all dimensions to influence your soul and body.

On the other hand, if you pray regularly in tongues, even if you don't clearly hear God, you will definitely find yourself *walking in the perfect will of God* for your life.

In the New Testament, Paul frequently uses the Greek word **hamartia** to define sin. This term when interpreted in English means, "missing the mark." What is missing the "mark" Paul refers to as sin? The mark could be missing the perfect will of God in your life. God might have called you to fulfill certain duties, but you actually missed doing them; for you are currently doing something else.

For example, there are people in businesses today who are supposed to be pastors. There are stationed pastors who are in fact called to be evangelists. There are people in politics who are supposed to be medical doctors, but they fail to take their positions and thus live in **hamartia**. They are in a great mess for they live outside the divine plan of God for their lives.

God might have placed your blessings in the area He called you to be, if you are not there then someone else can collect all the blessings meant for you. Don't blame God for missing the blessings meant for you. You have stationed yourself in a wrong place outside the perimeter of your destined calling.

For instance, when you are awarded a scholarship to

study in a certain specific university, your finances are sent direct to that institution. But if you decide to go to another institution on your own then you will miss your scholarship.

Jeremiah was called a prophet but he didn't know; he disputed his calling. (Jer. 1:5-6) He wanted to do something else.

If you pray regularly in tongues, the Spirit of God can *drive* you into the position or place God wants you to be— the perfect will of God meant for your life. Jude says, "But ye, beloved, building up yourselves on your most holy faith, praying in the Holy Ghost." (1:20)

Accomplishing Prayer

I want to touch on something that we often forget in prayer. Many of us are victim of this notion. It may be due to strict time scheduling or just apathy. If you have a burning desire to pray for specific issues that you feel God is placing in your heart, don't leave your prayers halfway, but rather finish praying until you are satisfied.

Whether you are praying in tongues or praying using your understanding, try to finish what you have started. I know of many friends who calculate how many minutes they would use for prayer and when the minutes are over they leave praying and do something else. Even waiting to hear from God is a waste.

In Matthew 26:38-48 we see Jesus praying until the "thought" in His heart was accomplished. He went to pray with a pain in heart (v.38) and when He came to check His disciples, they were asleep. He woke them up, challenged them and *went back* to pray for the second time since His prayer was yet incomplete. He came back and the thought still lingered in His mind, and so *He went again* for the third time to pray. (v.42) When it was complete He was then ready to face the adversary. (v.46)

The son of a well-known evangelist from the United States once revealed to Sid Roth on *It's Supernatural* that he had often watched his father praying in the house and when his prayer became so intense, instead of saying "amen" his father would take him to their farm where he would finish his prayer. He would wait in a distant watching his father. The father would pray until he was satisfied without thinking about the time.

Sometimes he would hear his father repeatedly talking to God and answering back. He would then start thanking God while speaking the revealed answers loudly several times. The result of that accomplished prayer was the establishment of Oral Roberts University by Oral Roberts.

Dr. David Yong Cho spoke on the same notion. He was praying with his pastors and after the conclusion he felt he wanted to pray some more. The group left but he stayed behind. He continued praying until he was satisfied—God finished speaking to him.

Don't cut your prayers short because of time. Move on until you feel you are satisfied. Daniel continued praying and fasting until Michael showed up to rescue the Messenger being blocked by the prince of Persia (satan) from bringing the answer to Daniel. If Daniel had cut short his praying and fasting, the Archangel Michael would not have been able to come to give Daniel God's answer. Daniel would have prayed but wouldn't have heard God's answer. (Dan. 10)

Similarly, when we are praying for people, especially those who are sick, we should not be ignorant about healing techniques.

Jesus came to the town of Bethsaida and a blind man was brought to Him for healing. (Mark 8:22-25) He took the blind man by the hand and led him out of the town. He spit on his eyes while touching them and asked the blind man what he saw, but the man said he saw "men as trees, walking." (v.24) That means the man was not completely healed. Jesus *again* touched his eyes and made him look up. At that time, He was totally restored (v.25) and was sent home rejoicing.

We see the persistence of healing that Jesus shows us so that we would follow it when encountering such challenges.

During deliverance times, sometimes evil spirits can pretend as if they are cast out completely but they want to deceive those ministers. Ask God to help you discern such tricks. Sometimes ministers like to provoke evil spirits and never finish what they have started. Accomplish what you have started in order to obtain results. Don't leave things partially complete.

REPLICATING TONGUES SPEAKERS

Replication in our context is the principle of reproducing and multiplying one's self in others. For example, if I am a successful businessperson and I put all my efforts into making others successful in the same business as myself, I am in fact replicating. I transfer the techniques, ideas and qualities that I have, to certain groups of people to make them successful.

In the church of Antioch believers were first called "Christians" by critics because they were seen as replica of Christ. (Acts 11:26) They acted, talked and walked like Christ. They were like "little Christs" and even accepted death due to their loyalty to their Redeemer. The unbelievers in Antioch sarcastically nicknamed them "Christians" to tease them for their Christ-like tendency.

This means that His chosen ones will exhibit the same qualities, approaches and secrets Jesus Christ used while on earth. He has chosen us to represent Him on earth. That is why believers in Christ are called *ambassadors* of Christ doing the same ministry of reconciliation as Christ did on earth. (2 Cor. 5:20)

Any gift God has blessed you with must be replicated in the lives of others. You must not keep them secret. Transfer these gifts to others, especially in your circle of influence. Paul invested all that he had in Timothy (and others). He confidently tells Timothy, "And the things you have heard me say in the presence of many witnesses entrust to reliable people who will also be qualified to teach others." (2 Tim 2:2 NIV) Who are your "Timothys" in whom you are investing yourself?

How can people "be qualified to teach others" about the infilling of the Holy Spirit with ability of speaking in tongues when they have not encountered the phenomenon? On Pentecost day only 120 people were baptized in the Holy Spirit but within a few minutes or hours 3,000 new tongues speakers were added. (Acts 2) It was because Peter didn't hide the gift in himself but with much pleading, he urged the onlookers to believe in Jesus Christ and receive the same gift the disciples had just received.

God loves people who are generous givers and hates mean people. Those who don't go out to entrust others with the gifts obtained from Christ are mean. They are sitting on what God just delegated for multiplication purposes. In due time we will be answerable before God. God says, "It is more blessed to give than to receive." (Acts 20:35) What do you give? You give what you already have! You can't give something you don't have.

Remember the story of the master who gave his servants talents to invest and two multiplied theirs but the third one hid the talent underground until the master came. The third servant was condemned for hiding his talent. (Matt. 25:14-30) When you invest, you do not expect to receive the same amount you invested; you expect to receive a profit. God expects a profit in the giftings He has invested in us. We should not sit on them.

There are people in the ministry who are very stingy despite the fact that God has blessed them with various spiritual resources worth being replicated. They want other people to buy those "resources" from them.

A woman recently asked a certain minister to pray for her. The minister told her he had the anointing of prosperity, so if the woman wanted answers to her prayer, she should give him $1,500 before praying for her. That minister referred to 1 Samuel 9:7 which says that people who consult seers would usually take something at hand. So he wanted that gift.

Is this a replicating notion? If Elijah was able to replicate himself in Elisha and imparted a double portion of anointing, we can learn from that. Replicate the gift of tongues in others. Teach and pray for "dry" believers to be "soaked" in the power of the Spirit to enable them to speak in tongues and do divine exploits.

Insurance companies understand the law of replication very well. If you become an insurance agent and you are licensed to distribute investment products, you are expected to duplicate yourself by recruiting more people in your business, teaching them the same principles you use so that they are able to work by themselves. You also advise them to recruit more people under them; and those who are recruited are taught to do the same. This is the principle of replication.

The more you build your "base shop" the more you will earn profit direct or indirectly.

In a simple way, when you help one believer to succeed in their Christian walk and that person goes on to bring more people to Christ, you will share in all their blessings. Daniel tells us that in replication, "they that be wise shall shine as the brightness of the firmament; and they that turn many to righteousness as the stars for ever and ever." (Dan. 12:3)

Take a moment to reflect on the people in the centers of your influence. Are they really appreciating you because you are replicating yourself in them positively? If not, it's never too late. You still have a chance!

CONCLUSION

We have now come to the conclusion of this book concerning the phenomenon of speaking in tongues with all its renderings. I hope you have greatly enjoyed reading and are encouraged to step forward to walk in the supernatural that you were created to perform.

You might have already been filled in the Holy Spirit and are able to speak in tongues. This book is saying you can grow even more in the things of the Spirit. Do something scriptural that you have never done before. You might also be born again but not activated your tongues gift. You have more knowledge now to seek Him with diligence.

Or else, you may be interested in the things of the Spirit but you are not sure whether you are born again or not. I want to encourage you that you still have a chance to repent and commit your life to Jesus Christ. The Apostle Peter told the people watching the happenings during Pentecost to repent and believe in Jesus Christ in order to receive the same gift of the Spirit the disciples had just received. He knew salvation was a prerequisite and foundational for all spiritual blessings from God.

The Bible says, "For whosoever shall call upon the name of the Lord shall be saved." (Rom. 10:13 NIV) How do you call on the name of the Lord to be saved? Verse nine of Romans gives us clear criteria on how to receive Jesus Christ as Lord and Savior. "If you *confess with your mouth* the Lord Jesus and *believe in your heart* that God has raised Him from the dead, you will be saved." (emphasis italicized)

You confess Jesus Christ using your mouth and believe the Lordship of Jesus Christ in your heart. The confession you make must come from your heart not from your mind. You must mean what you say. If you do, there will be a shift in your life. You have crossed from damnation into eternal life. After Christ comes into your heart to be your Lord and Savior, call on Him to bless you with the gift of tongues. You will receive what you desire because Jesus says so. (Mark 11:24)

Speaking in tongues is vital to our Christian walk because the utterance doesn't come from our mind but emanates from our spirit. (Rom. 8:26; 1 Cor. 14:14)

The mind is bypassed because of its "infirmity." The prayers that come from our mind don't comprehend heavenly things. The mind uses our experiences more than the voice and intent of God.

Not only does speaking in tongues avoid our mind but it also bypasses satan. The devil cannot understand what has been spoken in tongues because the message is coded. Only God is the one who knows what is spoken. Satan is always caught off guard because he cannot decode the codes of God in tongues. The more we pray in tongues the more we confuse satan and remove him from our sight.

When we speak in tongues we build ourselves up and our faith, vigor and thirst for God rise to a new level for the working of miracles. The Bible says, "He that speaketh in an unknown tongue edifieth himself." (1 Cor.14:4) When tongues are interpreted, the church will be edified and nonbelievers hearing them will be convicted to turn to Christ. How wonderful is our blessed Lord who has blessed us with all kinds of blessings in the heavenly places!

This book also explains the pivotal dynamics of speaking in tongues. The common tongue language which causes confusion to many Christians today is its *gibberish* utterances. Paul explained this in detail in 1 Corinthians 14. When we speak in tongues in a gibberish language unknown to us, satan and even the angels can do nothing about it unless God interprets for us what we are speaking.

Gibberish language is a "babbling" speaking without comprehensive expression. Humanly speaking, it sounds weird but builds up the one speaking. Paul tells the Corinthians that he speaks this kind of tongues more often than them all. (v.18) In fact in Athens Paul was called a "babbler" which indicates some unique trends he exercised in that place. (Acts 17:18)

We have also learned that speaking in tongues has diversities worth knowing. Some tongue languages are *articulate*—meaning the spoken knowledge is an actual language spoken by certain groups of people on earth. One example was during the Pentecost when the disciples of Jesus spoke languages known by the people around them. The hearers were convicted to repent and 3,000 new members joined the body of Christ. (Acts 2)

Some of the tongue languages are *wordless groans*. Romans 8:27 explains that the Holy Spirit prompts the speaking but in wordless groans which is "unuttered." This kind of prayer language is the highest level and we all need to reach to it. For instance, when you sleep and wake up you find yourself praying with groans. That is wonderful. The Spirit Himself intercedes for you.

We dealt in details about the ways to hear God when speaking in tongues. The book reveals some important ways to hear God since He uses our five senses to talk to us. I mean hearing, seeing, feeling/touching, smelling and tasting senses. God also drops messages into our inner beings in the form of random thoughts and random words. I gave many practical examples from the Bible, from other believers and my personal encounters. If we know and understand the Spirit's "urges" within us, interpreting our tongue language is as easy as understanding any other language we know.

Some people are not filled with the Holy Spirit and don't speak in tongues. Others have tried different ways to receive their gift but never received and feel uneasy or relegate themselves to the corner. Reread some of the best practical examples shown in this book on how to receive the gift of tongues. Seek the gift of tongues by faith and believe you will receive them because the Bible says you can.

If you do speak in tongues and operate in the supernatural, don't keep all these blessings to yourself. Impart them to others so that those will be able to also help others. Jesus has given you all these gifts for a purpose: to feed and tend His sheep. Those who operate in the fivefold ministry are encouraged to teach others (Eph. 4:11) and all believers are called royal priests. (1 Pet. 2:9)

Continue speaking in tongues often—in fact speak regularly so that you will be able to hear God clearly and walk according to the perfect will of God in your life. The Old Testament prophets were looking forward to what we have today. Daniel says, "They that be wise shall shine as the brightness of the firmament; and they that turn many to righteousness as the stars for ever and ever." (Dan. 12:3)

I want to conclude by giving you a chance to revive your spirit once more. Let the supernatural peace and love of God, which surpasses all human understanding, illuminate your mind and propel you to do the supernatural works with all diligence through the enablement of the Spirit of God in your life in the name of the Lord Jesus Christ. Shalom.

ABOUT THE AUTHOR

Peter Towongo is a pastor, author, teacher, motivator and mentor. Peter is the founding director of Compassion Ministries International and travels around Canada, United States, Israel and other parts of the world addressing critical issues affecting social and spiritual development of individuals.

After primary and secondary instructions, Peter attended Koboko Bible Training Centre (KBTC) and Alpha-Omega Seminary in Uganda jointly with Global University, USA. Peter studied courses on counselling psychology and education at Trinity Western University and The University of British Columbia, Canada.

Peter was born to South Sudanese parents and raised in church all his life. He was a missionary in Uganda, South Sudan and the Democratic Republic of Congo

Peter is the author of several inspirational books including *Power: 3 Steps to Kindle the Power Within You* and *Package of Salvation*. He is regularly sought for conferences, seminars, workshops and other notable gatherings including one-on-one.

www.petertowongo.com

BOOKS BY THE AUTHOR

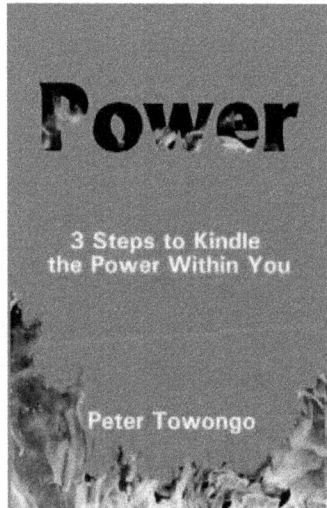

Do you know that everything you need in life is packed inside you? Perhaps you are currently desperate for wealth, peace, love, courage, health, eternal life and other bestowments. This book will help address your inner struggles and give you step-by-step guidelines to understand, recognize and kindle the power within you.

ISBN: 978-0-9949361-0-3 ~ eBook ~ paperback ~ 220 pages

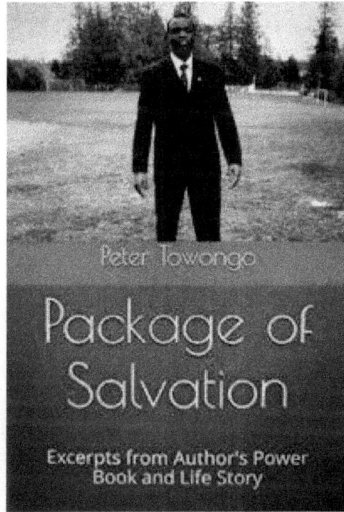

The ***Package of Salvation*** is a doorstep that will enable you to live a life worth meaningful both in the <u>now</u> and the <u>future</u> you will spend your eternity. This book reveals essential components of salvation prescribed by the eternal Creator for everyone to embrace. I have also included my "unusual" life story detailing the unfathomed power of God working in me thus making me who I am today.

ISBN: 978-0-9949361-3-4 ~ eBook ~ paperback

For additional copies of this book, testimonies,
or comments, please write to:

PETER TOWONGO

110 - 5377 201A Street

Langley BC V3A 1S7

CANADA

Email: info@petertowongo.com

Copies of this book can also be accessed online at:

www.petertowongo.com
www.compassionministry.org
www.amazon.com

www.ingramcontent.com/pod-product-compliance
Lightning Source LLC
Chambersburg PA
CBHW070348090426
42733CB00009B/1337